The disappointment: or, The force of credulity. A new American comic-opera, in three acts. By Andrew Barton, Esq. Second edition, revised and corrected, with large additions by the author. [Four lines of verse].

Thomas Forrest

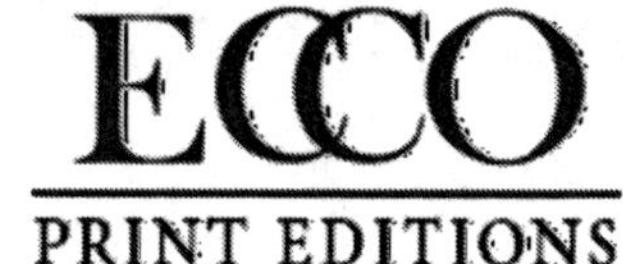

The disappointment: or, The force of credulity. A new American comic-opera, in three acts. By Andrew Barton, Esq. Second edition, revised and corrected, with large additions by the author. [Four lines of verse].

Forrest, Thomas
ESTCID: W030783
Reproduction from British Library
Without music. The authorship is disputed. Variously attributed to Andrew Barton (probably a pseudonym), John Leacock, and Thomas Forrest. The attribution to Forrest is most commonly accepted. Cf. the critical edition of this work, edited by David Mays (
Philadelphia : Printed for and sold by Francis Shallus no. 40, Vine-Street, M.DCC.XCVI. [1796].
iv, [3], 8-94, [2] p., [1] leaf of plates : ill. ; 12°

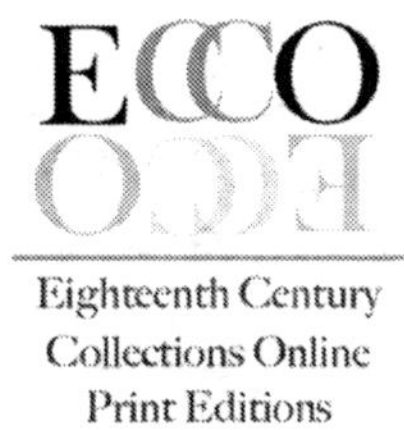

Gale ECCO Print Editions

Relive history with *Eighteenth Century Collections Online*, now available in print for the independent historian and collector. This series includes the most significant English-language and foreign-language works printed in Great Britain during the eighteenth century, and is organized in seven different subject areas including literature and language; medicine, science, and technology; and religion and philosophy. The collection also includes thousands of important works from the Americas.

The eighteenth century has been called "The Age of Enlightenment." It was a period of rapid advance in print culture and publishing, in world exploration, and in the rapid growth of science and technology – all of which had a profound impact on the political and cultural landscape. At the end of the century the American Revolution, French Revolution and Industrial Revolution, perhaps three of the most significant events in modern history, set in motion developments that eventually dominated world political, economic, and social life.

In a groundbreaking effort, Gale initiated a revolution of its own: digitization of epic proportions to preserve these invaluable works in the largest online archive of its kind. Contributions from major world libraries constitute over 175,000 original printed works. Scanned images of the actual pages, rather than transcriptions, recreate the works ***as they first appeared.***

Now for the first time, these high-quality digital scans of original works are available via print-on-demand, making them readily accessible to libraries, students, independent scholars, and readers of all ages.

For our initial release we have created seven robust collections to form one the world's most comprehensive catalogs of 18th century works.

Initial Gale ECCO Print Editions collections include:

History and Geography
Rich in titles on English life and social history, this collection spans the world as it was known to eighteenth-century historians and explorers. Titles include a wealth of travel accounts and diaries, histories of nations from throughout the world, and maps and charts of a world that was still being discovered. Students of the War of American Independence will find fascinating accounts from the British side of conflict.

Social Science
Delve into what it was like to live during the eighteenth century by reading the first-hand accounts of everyday people, including city dwellers and farmers, businessmen and bankers, artisans and merchants, artists and their patrons, politicians and their constituents. Original texts make the American, French, and Industrial revolutions vividly contemporary.

Medicine, Science and Technology
Medical theory and practice of the 1700s developed rapidly, as is evidenced by the extensive collection, which includes descriptions of diseases, their conditions, and treatments. Books on science and technology, agriculture, military technology, natural philosophy, even cookbooks, are all contained here.

Literature and Language
Western literary study flows out of eighteenth-century works by Alexander Pope, Daniel Defoe, Henry Fielding, Frances Burney, Denis Diderot, Johann Gottfried Herder, Johann Wolfgang von Goethe, and others. Experience the birth of the modern novel, or compare the development of language using dictionaries and grammar discourses.

Religion and Philosophy
The Age of Enlightenment profoundly enriched religious and philosophical understanding and continues to influence present-day thinking. Works collected here include masterpieces by David Hume, Immanuel Kant, and Jean-Jacques Rousseau, as well as religious sermons and moral debates on the issues of the day, such as the slave trade. The Age of Reason saw conflict between Protestantism and Catholicism transformed into one between faith and logic -- a debate that continues in the twenty-first century.

Law and Reference
This collection reveals the history of English common law and Empire law in a vastly changing world of British expansion. Dominating the legal field is the *Commentaries of the Law of England* by Sir William Blackstone, which first appeared in 1765. Reference works such as almanacs and catalogues continue to educate us by revealing the day-to-day workings of society.

Fine Arts
The eighteenth-century fascination with Greek and Roman antiquity followed the systematic excavation of the ruins at Pompeii and Herculaneum in southern Italy; and after 1750 a neoclassical style dominated all artistic fields. The titles here trace developments in mostly English-language works on painting, sculpture, architecture, music, theater, and other disciplines. Instructional works on musical instruments, catalogs of art objects, comic operas, and more are also included.

biblioLife
old books. new life.

THE

DISAPPOINTMENT;

OR, THE

FORCE OF CREDULITY.

A NEW COMIC OPERA,

IN THREE ACTS.

BY ANDREW BARTON, Esq.

Second Edition, revised and corrected, with large additions, by the Author.

Enchanting gold! thou oft conspire to blind
Man's erring judgment, and misguide the mind;
In search of thee, the [illegible] worldling goes,
Nor danger fears, tho' [illegible] of [illegible] oppose.

PHILADELPHIA.

PRINTED FOR AND SOLD BY

FRANCIS SHALLUS, No. 40, VINE-STREET.

MDCCXCVI.

PREFACE.

THE following local piece (The Disappointment, or, the Force of Credulity,) was originally written for the amusement of myself and a few of my particular friends, who were pleased to signify their approbation of it in such a manner, as to engross a considerable part of the conversation of all ranks of people, who expressed their desire to see it and have it published.—Under these circumstances, I was greatly at a loss how to proceed, (as I could discover little merit in it and never intended it for the press) I was loth to expose it to the criticisms of critics in dramatic or scholastic knowledge, to ridicule my ignorance, or condescend to those, who I thought were no better judges than myself, and who might, perhaps out of compliment or flattery to me, or to gratify their own desires, have represented it in a more favourable light than it really deserves.—Conscious therefore of its insufficiency, I determined to excuse myself to all, and in this determination persisted for some time, till at length wearied out with fresh and repeated solicitations I was obliged to surrender on the following stipulations.

1. The infant state of dramatic compositions in America.
2. The necessity of contributing to the entertainment of the city.
3. To put a stop (if possible) to the foolish and pernicious practice of searching after supposed hidden treasure.*

These terms, I have with reluctance been forced to submit to, I am therefore obliged to assure the public, that the piece is founded on fact, transacted near this city not long since and is recent in the memory of thousands, and for the truth of which I appeal to my fellow citizens.

* Many people to this day, are possessed with a foolish notion of the Pirates burying money along the river sides, and are so infatuated with the hopes of obtaining it, that they neglect their business by day with the thoughts of it, by which means their families suffer, and at night, like so many mischievous [illegible], spoil the meadows and banks to the very great injury of their respective owners.

But in order to give strangers, and others unacquainted with the story, some idea of [illegible] the following short history is thought necessary.

The scheme was planned by four humorous gentlemen, Hum Parchment, Quadrant and Rattle [illegible] themselves, and found a way to try at length the credulity and the love of money [illegible] carry men.—

In order [illegible] the scheme in execution they framed a plan [illegible] money or hidden treasure, and to gloss the matter over, [illegible] to the purpose and pitched upon two suitable old fellows, Wallball and Raccoon (as principal dupes, with others who had been at times on several digging excursions) to try the success of their scheme, and put (if possible) a final stop to such ridiculous practices in future, which had the desired effect. The moral shews the folly of an over credulity and desire of money, and how apt men are (especially old men) to be unwarily drawn into such schemes, where there is but a shadow of gain, and concludes with love and virtue well rewarded, and these observations, that mankind ought to be contented with their respective stations, to follow their different vocations with honesty and industry, the only sure and reputable way to gain riches.

I do not figure to myself the least advantage accruing from it but the satisfaction of contributing my mite to stop the current of such folly.—Such as it is, I submit to the public for their sanction or condemnation, and should any merit appear in the performance, I shall not vainly attribute it to myself, but place it to the credit of mere chance.

I am the public's most

obedient, humble devoted

and faithful servant,

ANDREW BARTON.

PROLOGUE.

THO' distant far, from fam'd Britannia's isle,
Where comic scenes call critics forth to smile,
Our artless muse, hath made her first essay,
T' instruct and please you with a modern play
Theatric bus'ness was, and still should be
To point out vice in its deformity,
Make virtue fair! shine eminently bright,
Rapture the breast and captivate the sight!
No matter which the pulpit or the stage,
Condemn the vice and folly of the age,
These are our boast and on sure ground we stand
Plead virtue's cause, throughout this infant land.
We mount the stage and lend an helping hand.
Wits, fools, a knave and conjuror to night
The objects make both of your ears and sight,
A band of dupes are humm'd with idle schemes,
Quit solid sense for airy golden dreams
Who boldly venture on enchanted ground,
And dig in mystic mud, no treasure found,
Still fondly hope, to plunder that old thief
BLACKBEARD! who plunder'd thousands, pirate chief!
Till disappointed, tho' they labour'd hard
For shadows, stones, and anguish, their reward!
Our flatt'ring muse thinks she's some merit gain'd
Pursuing truth and things like truth, well feign'd.
The subject suited to our present times
No person's touch'd, altho' she lash their crimes,
Nor gall, nor venom tincture her design
But gay good humour, breathe in ev'ry line.
If you condemn her,—she for censure stands;
But if applaud!—then thund'ring clap your hands!

DRAMATIS PERSONÆ.

MEN.

Hum, - -	A Tavern-keeper.	Humourists.
Parchment, -	A Scrivener.	
Quadrant, - -	A mathematical instrument maker.	
Rattletrap, -	A supposed conjuror.	
Raccoon, - -	An old debauchee.	Dupes.
Washball, - -	An avaracious old barber.	
Trushoop, -	A Cooper.	
Buckram, - -	A Taylor.	
Trowell, -	A Plaisterer.	
Meanwell, - -	A young gentleman in love with *Washball's* niece.	
Topinlift, - -	A Sailor.	
Spitfire, - -	An old Artillery man, assistant to *Rattletrap*.	
Old Gabriel, -	Servant to *Washball*.	
Terrance, -	Servant to *Trushoop*	

Collector, Taylors, Watchman, Blackbeard's ghost, &c. &c.

WOMEN.

Mrs Trowell, - Wife to *Trowell*.

Mrs Trushoop, - Wife to *Trushoop*.

Miss Lucy, - Washball's niece in love with *Meanwell*.

Moll Placket, - A woman of the town in keeping by *Raccoon*.

Dolly, - - Servant to *Mrs. Trushoop*.

THE

DISAPPOINTMENT;

OR, THE

FORCE OF CREDULITY.

ACT I.

SCENE I.—A Tavern; Sign of the Tun.

Scene opens and discovers HUM, PARCHMENT, *and* QUADRANT, *seated at a table, with wine and glasses.*

(PARCHMENT *pouring out a glass of wine, sings.*)

SONG I.

COME now my boys, let's jovial be,
The cash we ll soon disclose,
And spurn at sneak.ng poverty,
Tho Gorgons d're ' oppose.
The joyful night draws on apace,
Each moment joy inspires '
Whilst steady hope in ev ry face,
Add fa th to our desires.

We soon can face the rich and great,
(Whose supercilious squint,
Like Basilisks oft made us quake)
Or else the devil's in t '—
But stop ye sons of flash and mire,
Ye sons of projects rare !
If disappointed we retire,
Faith ' then,—we re as we were.

Sing tantara rara, fools all, fools all, fools all, Sing tantara rara, fools all, fools all, Sing tantara rara, fools all

Quad. Well tim'd at the opening of the ball. He he he!

Hum. Come success to us (*all drink success*) Well gentlemen how goes our scheme?—Have you made any new proselytes since our last meeting!

Hum. Why really, while credulity and the love of money prevail, I think it no merit to make proselytes of one half the town, but that you know, is not our purpose, we only want to draw in four or five of the most credulous, some of whom have actually been engaged in vain, visionary, and fruitless schemes of money digging to the great prejudice of their families and injury of their neighbours, and still entertain the most sanguine hopes of making their fortunes, at one slap, one of those odd nights by finding the lucky spot.—I baited the hook for old Soap-suds, he gap'd, snap'd, and swallow'd it as voraciously as a cringing courtier would a pension,—As for Raccoon, I just threw out a few hints, he sagaciously discovered (as he thought) the foundation and soon raised an imaginary fabric.

Quad. Oh!—if he smells money, as great a coward as they say he is, he'd venture to the gates of h—ll for it. He, he, he!

Hum. I've hitherto kept him in suspence, he haunts me like a ghost, he thinks something but knows nothing,—he'll be here presently, and I have contriv'd matters so, that he shall make the discovery himself.

Quad. Very good,—so far we have sailed propitiously, and I have not been idle, for I've drawn in Buckram, Trushoop, and Trowell, they are perpetually at my house—I can scarce do a stroke of work for one or other of them—I wish the matter speedily settled, for faith! they're so elevated, I'm afraid they'll run crazy. He, he, he! Trushoop talks of building a chappel at his own expence and of employing a score or two of priests to keep up a continual rotation of prayers for the repose of the souls of those poor fellows who buried the money. As for Buckram he intends to knock off bus'ness, go to London and purchase a title. He, he, he! they'll all be here in half an hour.

Parch. The devil!—Then I suppose they'll not be in a humour for work, till this affair is over—I'd some thoughts of a new suit of cloathes, but I must drop them, till these chimeras are out of Buckram's brain.

Hum. That's the only reason, why I want the business dispatched, for, tho' I like the diversion, I would'nt hurt their families—Oh! I'd like to have forgot—Washibal in particular is so full of sanguinity, on account of the treasure, that it has quite renovated him, perfectly grateful and so generous as to dub me a bashaw! by making me a present of a magnificent new wig of three tails. Ha, ha, ha!

Parch. The devil he has? Ha, ha, ha!—would better had one of mine, then you would have been a Bashaw of nine tails at once. Ha, ha!

Hum. No, no, three will do pretty well for a beginning. I've not quite so much ambition yet; he told me that he was sure when we got the money, I should be chosen President of the United States, or chief counsellor at law, at least, and if only the latter, three tails you know will be quite sufficient. Ha, ha!

Quad. True,—gratitude and generosity in the superlative! a rare example of faith and good works united.

Hum. Very rare indeed—tho' 'tis but temporary, we shall soon see Messrs Faith and Good Works at variance.

Quad. Very soon! very soon! they are but short liv'd, he, he, he! but Mr. Parchment, have you prepar'd the papers?

Parch. Yes, yes, I have em in my pocket.

Quad. Do let's see em, for they are the foundation of our undertaking.

Parch. (*pulling them out*) here they are, placed in regular order and inclosed in a letter to Mr. Hum.

Hum. Aye, aye, let's see; (*reads*) the letter will do to a tittle, but what the devil's this ancient, worm-eaten piece?

Parch. That's the will, authenticated and ratified.

Quad. Ratified with the devil to it. He, he, he! why they've knaw'd the one half up!

Parch. So much the better, the greater the deception.

Hum. Ha, ha! Why it looks as old as if it had been preserved in the temple of Apollo, or the tower of Babel!

Quad. Egad! you might have said Noah's Ark at once. He, he, he! for it looks old enough,—and pray what's this other weather beaten piece!

Parch. Why that's the draft of the place, together with the memorandum signed by the officers present, at the time the money, &c &c. were deposited, I've had them all these three weeks smoaking up the chimney

Quad. Faith I thought so! for I took them for flitches of Bacon. He, he, he! they have only the appearance of genuine antiquity, or baconosity. *(sings.)*

SONG II.

In all the town there's none like you
When you're on mischief bent sirs,
With pen and ink, one well can write
What you do both intent sirs.
Its you my boys, its you can do it,
Parchment you're my darling,
Raccoon may curse and Washball burst,
We value not their snarling
Tol, de rol, &c.

Hum. Very good, very good,—well I must take them into my care, as they are directed to me, *(gathers up the paper.)*—but I wonder what detains Jack Rattletrap?

Quad. Oh! I'll be bound for his appearance—I just came from his house and left him poring over the cant of Hudibras and Sydrophel, in order to furnish himself with a set of hard superfroilical, callepophricating words, which added to his knowledge in the mathematics, will completely qualify him for a modern conjuror.—but, here he comes!—talk of the devil and his imps appear,—as the saying is. He, he, he!

(Enter RATTLETRAP *singing.)*

SONG III.

Behold you my magical phiz
How solemn and sober I look:
Here, here my good friends, here is,
My brass bound magical book.
This book many wonders contain,
'Twould deceive the devil himself,
And puzzle a conjuror's brain,
Who has got no more sense than an elf.
Who has, &c.

Parch. Excellentissimo faith! Ha, ha! We began to look for you with impatience, are you almost prepared for your office?

Rat. Yes, dress and books are already provided, but for apparatus I must apply to Mr. Quadrant.

Quad. Yes, yes, I'll cut you a hazel rod off our cherry-tree, a magnet, nocturnal, telescope, spy-glass, and forestaff, shall be all ready, also a curious piece of antiquity, of full as much virtue as Fortunatus's cap. He, he, he! its nothing less than my great, great, great, great, grand-mother's quilted night-cap. He, he, he! and I can furnish you as Hudibrass says, with a—

Moon dial and Napier's bones
With store of constellation stones

He, he, he! But say, have you seen the papers?

Rat. Yes, yes, I saw them this morning at Mr. Parchment's office—but hark ee,—we want a fifth person to act as a familiar spirit, or demi devil.

Hum. Leave that to me,—I'm acquainted with an old artillery-man, who told me his father was a bombardier, that he himself was begot and born in the large mortar piece at Gibraltar, and that when only three years of age, the commanding officer (lord Something) taking a fancy to him and determining to make him truly a soldier, order'd him to be ramm'd in, and fir'd out of the mortar-piece, and he was blown over into the Spanish lines, and that he received not the least hurt, only a little marked with gunpowder.—He's a snug, hickory faced, dry dog, the most finished fellow in the world for this sort of sport,—he was also in the Carthagena expedition and would make nothing of cracking with his teeth, (like hazle nuts) and swallowing two or three bomb-shells every morning before breakfast [out of bravado only]—the devilishest fellow you ever saw,—but, poor fellow! he's lost most of his teeth by it.—I'll introduce him to you; with his assistance and a proper habit, you'll cut as droll a figure as old Merlin himself.

Quad. Well said, he, he, he! that's a hum with the devil to it superlatively hyperbolical faith! no wonder he's lost some of his teeth, he, he, he! a truly eccentric genius.

Rat. Excellent ha, ha! Introduce him by all means, he's the very identical devil I want, I love such a superlative devil! —I'll soon make him a super-superlative devil, we may then defy the power of Lucifer, Belzebub and the whole hoſt of devils united. Ha ha, ha!—As to the loſs of ſome of his teeth, it's a matter of no great conſequence, as we ſhall only want him to chew a few fire balls. Ha! ha! now and then.—But we muſt have a place provided for his reception under ground.—Mr. Quadrant and myſelf will ſee that done—drop the converſation here comes old Raccoon.

(*Enter* RACCOON.)

Rac. Your ſerbent gentlemen, brudder Hum, and brudders all I'm berry glad to ſee you all well.

Parch. Leave ceremonies brother Raccoon and take hold of the bottle (*drinks.*)

Hum. Gentlemen, I muſt beg your patience a few minutes, I'll be with you ſhortly. (*Exit Hum.*

[*As he went out he purpoſely dropp'd the papers, Raccoon pick'd them up, ſtepp'd aſide, and look'd over them.*]

Rac. (*Aſide*) Hah! brudder Hum hab I found you ſecret? I tought dere was ſumting in de wind, dis is a lucky bout, dad I'll keep deſe papers—dey ſhan't hab dem, widout dey gib me de ſhare. (*He crams them in his pocket and ſits down.*)

(*Re-enter* HUM, *looking confuſed.*)

Hum. Did you ſee any thing of a bundle of papers gentlemen?

Parch. No, I ſaw none.

Quad. Nor I.—What papers are they?

Hum. Zounds!—If you've got them, don't keep me in ſuſpence!

Rac. Upon my honor, I ſaw nothing of them.

Rac. What was dey about brudder Hum?

Hum. About, Zounds! they are papers of the utmoſt conſequence, of ineſtimable value—pray put me out of my pain, if you have them—if they're loſt, we're ruined—you're each of you as much intereſted in the recovery of them as *myſelf.*—for God's ſake! gentlemen look about. (*All riſe ſhake their clothes and ſearch about.*) Oh! that I had kept them to myſelf when I had them ſafe! fool that I was (*ſtamps about the ſtage and wrings his hands*) what ſhall I do?

Parch. There are no ſigns of them Mr. Hum.

Rat. Not the leaſt.

Hum. Then we're ruined [*Clapping his hands, &c. &c.*] and our ſcheme is abortive—if they are not here the damn'd waiter muſt have pick'd my pocket when he brought up the wine—damn the villain. [*Rings the bell.*]

Wait. (*Below.*) Coming ſir.

(*Enter* WAITER, WASHBALL, TRESHOOT, BUCKRAM, *and* TROWELL.)

Hum. You ſcoundrel, where's the papers you took?

Wait. Sir, I didn't take any.

Hum. You lie you raſcal!

Wait. I——I——

Waſh. What's the matter! what's the matter Mr. Hum?

Hum. We're undone! the villain has ſtole my papers —

Waſh. What papers? deliver the papers you dog! (*Lifts up his cane.*)

Wait. Upon my honor and ſoul gentlemen, I ſaw no papers at all.

Traſ. Damn your honor youſelf—I hope its no defence, gentlemen.

Buck. Onor!—what, a waiter in a tavern have onor!

Quel. His countenance condemns him.

Hum. You raſcal, I'll ſend for a conſtable, you ſhall be hang'd you villain.

Wait. For God's ſake! gentlemen, hear me! hear me!

Hum. (*Rings the bell.*) Who waits below there!

Traſ. O you tief of de world, when I fiſh for the devil, I'll bate my hook wid you.

Buck. Gin Ize gang to him, Ize—

Hum. A conſtable—a conſtable below there!

Wait. O Lord! O Lord! Oh! Oh! Oh!

Buck. Produce the pappers this eenſtant, or by Saint Andra Ize ſacrafeeſe ye! [*He ſeizes and ſhakes him.*]

Wait. Have mercy on me—don't kill me!

Waſh. Kill the dog!—kill him! kill him! [*Strikes him with his cane.*]

Wait. (*On his knees*) As I hope for mercy I'm innocent

Buck. Ye've but ane moment to live, deliver! deliver ye dug ye, or I'ze cut your damn'd thro'!

Trow. Hold your hand Mr. Buckram—let's search him.

Trus. Let me come to the flutberdegullion and I'll skin him like a Munster potatoe.

Rac. Come gentlemen be merciful—don't kill de poor fellow, search him. [*They search him but find none.*]

Hum. They're not about him—Zounds! what shall we do? (*Aside.*) violent measures won't avail, we must bribe him—come my lad, hearkee! be ingenuous with us, they're of no value to you, but of infinite consequence to us and if you'll produce them, we'll give you something handsome, and nothing more sha'll be said about them.

Wait. Sir, Sir!

Hum. Perhaps I've drop'd them—do my lad step down and look about.

Wait. I will indeed Sir. [*Exit Waiter.*

Hum. O most unfortunate affair!—how strange are the vicissitudes of human life?—one moment raised to the highest pinnac'e of human felicity, the next, sunk to the lowest pit of disappointment, and despair!—alas! alas! how cruel is my fate?—how—

Parch. Don't let us despair, Mr. Hum—perhaps—

Hum. Undone! inevitably undone! ruined!—past redemption! my hopes are fled!

Rac. Come, come budder Hum, make yourself easy, I did pick up de papers at de door.

Hum. Gracious fortune!

Rac. Budder Hum dropp'd dem as he goed out.

Hum. How thankful ought—

Rac. I did see de contents of dem—here dey are—(*Gives the papers.*)

Hum. O blessed papers!—once more—

Rac. And I hope you will let me come in for de share.

Hum. Certainly,—I am almost overcome with joy!—it affects me more than the most poignant grief I ever yet experienced, yet, however, I may be rejoiced at the recovery of the papers, I must say brother Raccoon, your imprudence, caution, and jealousy in detaining them so long, when you saw the anxiety of my soul, during the severe trial, was to say no worse, extremely cruel and unkind—However I impute it not to a sinister or dishonest motive but, rather to a thoughtless curiosity as to the consequences, being fully convinced of the generosity of your disposition and well knowing the best of men, do not at all times act wisely.

Wash Ah! Mr. Raccoon, it was very foolish of you, god knows what I suffer'd too—O dear!—what a pesterment I was in—but I charitably hope you had no selfish views in it—indeed I do

Rac. No upon my honour, I hab not Mr Washball, I only did it for fun or de want of tought.

Wash Devilish fun!—children's play—worse than shooting, firebrands, arrows, and death, to throw me into such a flusteration, Oh! dear Oh!—

(Trushoop *sings.*)

SONG IV.

You seem in a flutter
And pray what's the matter
  Now, now wid you all, now, now wid you all.
And can't you be azy
And not be so crazy
  Dear Master Washball, dear Master Washball.

Now the papers are found,
And all safe and sound
  And can't you be quiet, and can't you be quiet.
By my sowl! an I'm tir'd
And almost expir'd
  To hear such a riot, to hear such a riot.

What wou'd you have more
You son of fourscore?
  Hoot leave off your bawling, hoot leave off, &c.
Sit down and be azy
And no longer taze me
  Wid your caterwauling, wid your caterwauling.

If money you're wanting
Why leave off your grunting,

You scul'on curmudgeon, you scullion curmudgeon.
Since the money's in store,
What would you have more,
You slubberdegullion, you slubberdegullion.

Hum. Aye indeed we had all like to have been frustrated, come sit down gentlemen, we ought to be sincerely thankful the papers are safe. *(All sit down.)*

Parch. *(To Washball)* What can those papers mean?

Wash. Oh dear! Oh dear! how my heart beats for joy!

Trus. So do mine, I tought it would tump my liver out

Buck. Troth an I had na been stapp'd, I shou'd ha cut the waiter's throt, Ize g'ad ye prevented me, let's ca him up and gie him sumthing.

Trow. Aye do!—poor dog he was terribly frighten'd

Hum. Really, no wonder! I was much enraged at him—poor fellow. *(Rings the bell.)*

(Re enter WAITER.*)*

Wait. Did you call gentlemen?

Buck. Weel lad, we've foond the pappers, and here's sumthing to mak ye ameends for the freight ye got *(Gives him money)* and meend ye tell na ane, but keep it till yoursel lad.

Wait. I will Sir—Thankee kindly Sir—God bless your honor, —Thank your honor. *[Bowing.]*

Wash. Aye, Aye, a close tongue makes a wise head—remember that young man *[Gives money.]*.

Wait. I will Sir—heaven bless your honor, *(As he goes out bowing, the others throw money after him he picks it up)* the lord prosper you gentlemen!—heaven preserve your honors—*[Bowing]* thank your kind honors. *[Aside]* Faith and its no bad collection, I should like such another flourish very well *[Exit Wait.*

Parch. *(To Trushoop)* I say Mr. Trushoop, what are the contents of those papers?

Trush. The devil a hare do I know about it, at all, at all.

Hum. Well gentlemen, I look upon you all to be men of honor, I suppose most of you are not altogether strangers to the busin ss in agitation, you've all in miniature been informed of it, except Mr. Parchment and Mr. Trowell who are present and shall soon be informed.

Parch. *(Starting up suddenly)* Gentlemen, I expected when

I was invited here, it was to take a cheerful glaſs with my friends, I had no idea of a ſecret to be divulged, not I—and I earneſtly requeſt that, if it is any ſcheme, plot, aſſociation or combination, machination, contrivance, ſecret conclave, cabal, privy conſpiracy, rout, riot, rebellious meeting or unlawful aſſembly—In fine, if it is any thing againſt the illuſtrious Preſident of the United States, or of the Society of Cincinnati, whom God preſerve!—the honorable the Vice Preſident of the honorable Senate—the honorable the Senate collectively, or individually,—The honorable the Houſe of Repreſentatives of the United States that ſtanding Bulwark of American freedom, in Congreſs aſſembled, or not aſſembled, or either of them,—The honorable the Secretary of State.—The honorable the Secretary of the treaſury,—the honorable the Secretary at war—the honorable the chief juſtice of the United States—the honorable the aſſociate judges in their judicial capacity or, otherwiſe—the honorable the Attorney general of the United States—The Right Reverend the biſhops and clergy of the United States of all denominations, whether in church, or out of it—the conſtitution, laws and government under which we live—to be brief—I ſay gentlemen, if it is any ſcheme, plot, aſſociation combination, machination, contrivance, ſecret conclave, cabal, privy conſpiracy, rout, riot, rebellious meeting or unlawful aſſembly as I ſaid once more, keep it to yourſelves, don't let me know a tittle of it—I waſh my hands of it—for if I know it, I'll be a firſt witneſs againſt you, as I profeſs myſelf a worthy Citizen a true republican a man of honor and a gentleman by birth and education—I'll immediately go to the Attorney-General, lodge an information againſt you and hang you every mother's ſon!

Waſh. Dear, dear ſir! don't think of ſuch a thing.

Parch. Don't tell me ſir (*Raiſing his voice*)

Waſh. Sir! Sir!—you've known me theſe many, many long years, I've always lived peaceably and never was concerned in any of thoſe diſturbances you have mentioned as all my neighbours can teſtify,—Lord! Lord! Mr. Parchment—

Parch. Mr Waſhball I've nothing to charge you with—but, Sir, my ſuſpicions are—

Waſh. Are what?—Lord! Sir, what?

Parch Sir, it carries an inſidious countenance!—a damn'd de- [illegible] look—

Wig. Come go ... —speak to him fomebody—do! do! Oh dear! Oh! I'm out of breath.

Rat. Sir I believe there's none in this company but what are as true republicans as yourself.

Buck. By my fawl mon! an I ha as great a regard for the ... Illustrious President of the United States as ye ha there's ... travels in America mon.

Parch. I hope there are not—never ... he's, it has a Guy Faux appearance a ... ed romantic look.

Trom. How can you say so?

Quad. I'm furious ... Mr. Parchment.

Trus. The devil burn me, but ... I ...

Parch. I tell you gentlemen, ... Gunpowder, treason, blood, affassination, ... laughter, ... and murder.

Wig. I'll give you my bond for five hundred pounds, it is no such thing indeed, indeed it an't Mr. Parchment.—Oh dear! speak to him fomebody.

Buck. Deel damme mon, ... again and by St. Andrew, I'ze cut aff your head.

Parch. I'm not to be frightened by you Mr. Buckram damme Sir you're a ...

Ham. (*Aside.*) Moderate your passion Mr. Buckram, don't be too rash, let me speak to him.—I hope Mr. Parchment you won't suppose any of us capable of conspiring against the government no Sir!—I answer for all present (you ...) the United States ha not more faithful republicans— ... business that you were desired to attend upon here this evening I ... communicate—if you'll hear—but, if not—why, Sir—

Trom. Aye, do hear—if you don't ... you can be off, as well as me ...

Trus. Arrah my dear! ... have a little patience an we'll tell you, all an more too, honey.

Buck. Deel damme mon, If you won't hear, ye may e'en gang aboot your business.

Rat. I think him totally unworthy of any communication whatever.

Quad. Your behaviour is very extraordinary—let me tell you Mr. Parchment—I ... expected the like from you.

P ... —

...

o t the company and make what use of our proceed gs you t ik proper—we can a f ve. for ourselves.

Truf. Yes and hang us too, and then turn States evidence, would not you?

Larch. You being my old friends, I still regard you, therefore I drop these thoughts. I would not injure your persons or famil—I confess I was over zealous, when I made use of the expression.

Buck. Domme mon and that's mon feek

Kar. Come come, Mr. Parchment consider

Trow. Hear Sir, hear!

Hum. I promise you you'll have no cause to repent of it? 'tis on of pure regard to you, we gave you the invitation. [*Aside*] I could wish him to be one of us he'd be of infinite service.

Purch. On condition it is none of those things I have mentioned I am ready to hear.

Hum. I give you my honour and the sacred word of a mason if it is not, and here my hand upon it. [*Shakes hands.*]

Larch. I'm satisfy'd Mr. Hum.

Trow. Now this is clever, it's just like brethren dwelling together in unity.

Truf. Faith an it is—it looks well on our side again—by my faul an its for all the world now, like too hoores fighting and quarreling and soon make it up agai

Trow. A bad beginning sometimes makes a good ending.

Truf. That's true for you my dear. (*To Parchment*) mind that honey

Hum. Well silence gentlemen!—you must know then that I have very unexpectedly and to my very great joy, received a letter from my young sister in law in England, who is heiress to the famous Captain Bluebeard [*of bl ssed memory*] inclosing sundry papers, such as, original letters, a will, a power of attorney plans charts drafts and memoranda ount of a vast quantity of of treasure, &c. &c. that was buried by the pirates, about a century ago here in America and these are the papers gentlemen, please to look over them. [*They look over them.*]

Parch. Ah!—I beg you ten thousand pardons gentlemen—since it is an affair of this nature I join you with all my heart.

Truf. The devil doubt you man you're welcome

Kar. (*Pointing to one of the papers in Parchments hand*) What ca ?—do Mr Parchment read it—I can't see without my spectacle

Wash. Aye do read it, let us hear every thing

Parch. May I presume to read it Mr Hum ?

Hum. By all means, sir—as you're a gentleman of the quill a chirographist, you're used with these out fashion'd writings

Parch. Arroque Dominus ... Why I find — but I'll omit the preamble, it's a particular account of the treasure. It is as follows ... gold, ... Portugal pieces, ... Spanish pistoles, ... 73 ... of gold, 1 small box of diamonds, ... pieces of ... of Mexico, ... large boxes of pearls ... weight ... and the picture of his holiness pope Gregory ... in a frame of solid gold embellished with ... and inclosed in a gold box.

His infrument ... signed by

Edward Teach, alias Blackbeard -	Captain
Moses Brum ... e - - - -	1st Lieutenant.
... an Rucbe ... - - - -	2d Lieutenant.
Judas ... - - - -	Gunner.
Harry Split-throat - - - -	Boatswain.
Henery Hatedevil - - -	C...

Wash. Oh what a treasure!—what do you think of our project now ... Mr Parchment, he! he! he

Parch. I here ... remember ... I have no concern in such a project, ... occasion

Trus. ... any ... from ... ?

Parch. Oh no—god forbid Mr ... —for ...

Trus. ... Mr Gunpowder and blood

Hum. Ha! ha! ... —well here's enough for us all

Trus. ... could but get ... it

Quad. He! he! he!

Par.—Ha! ha! ha!

R. ... my ... we a mean ... con ... ion

an keep the shop—bolt out at the window

Wash. I'll have no more. I'll keep my hands out of the fields.

Rat. Dis will make me cut de figure in life and appear in de world wid de proper importance and den I'll do someting for posterity.

Trus. For my part, I'm not boast about it.---But the world shall see I'll put it to a good use.

Rat. Very good, very good gentlemen but let us proceed to business.—Our work must be carried on with Secrecy and dispatch.—Beside it will be attended with some trifling expence at the outset, for refreshments &c. &c.—I believe it will be necessary to appoint Mr. Parchment our Secretary and Treasurer, if it be agreeable to him.

All say. With all our hearts!

Parch. [*Rising up*] Gentlemen!—you have already laid me under many obligations and these appointments I look upon as an infallible proof of your esteem—I accept of them with gratitude and heartily thank you for your kind information and admission into your company, and the great confidence, you have (so unworthily) reposed in me, and you may depend upon the most religious secrecy, faithfulness, accuracy, dispatch, and punctuality.

Trus. Well now an that's a very fine speech! by my soul an father Murphy (or Murtagh O Lowery), never made a better.

Ham. Ha! Ha!—a queer dog.

Quid. What sum do you imagine Mr. Rattletrap, will be necessary for each to deposit?

Rat. O trifling trifling, I suppose about half a Joe per man for the present, for tavern expences and a few fees.

Rat. Before I make use of my art, to discover this treasure, I must insist that each of you go to Mr. Parchment's office and be sworn to secrecy and honesty to each other and there deposit your respective quotas.

All. Agreed! agreed!

Ham. Well gentlemen it grows late,—let's break up for the present. I expect to see you all to-morrow evening, at six o'clock, mean while let it remain a profound secret—remember you are now going to be sworn, so don't let your nearest friends, or even your wives know it!

Trus. That's true for you—let me alone for that, honey!

Trow. Not a soul living shall get a word out of me.

(*All rise.*)

(PARCHMENT *sings.*)

SONG V.

Now let us join hands and unite in this cause
'Tis glorious gold, that will gain us applause,
How happy are we! with such treasure in store!
We'll clothe all the naked and feed all the poor.

We'll clothe, &c.

How happy for me, to this country I came?
You all my dear friends now can witness the same,
In wealth to abound Oh! the thought is most sweet,
No more will I write for one farthing a sheet.

No more, &c.

Bus. Now my braw lads, au stand true,

Truf. Ara faith! will we that's true for you.

[*Exeunt.*

SCENE II. *As away.*

Watchman. (*Going his round*) Pa phast thurtee un glock, un rainy mo-o-or ning.——

(*Enter* TRUSHOOP, *on the opposite side.*)

Truf. Fa h an that fellows out it—by my soul! but I believe Noah's Ark never rained harder.—Now, an what the devil will I be after saying to my wife?—an what excuse will I make?—by my sowl! an she looked as black as a Carolina tunder squall at me toder night, when I cummed home in the morning—By the holy Store! an I'm very afeard to timp at the dure—but I can't stand this way in the morning, lying out in the cowl rain all night—by my sowl! and this sitting up all night will be the det of me—faith an I'll tell her all the secret—but that won't do nather for I'm how sworn, an I'll not sell my sowl to the devil for a handful of sew dings—Well if I had the wisdom of the holy St Patrick—St. Dominic—St. Kullumkill—Murtogh O Laferty—the venerable Labre an all the pish fhaints of Ireland, I would'nt be able to tell what to do,—but faith an I must cum in somehow, or toder. (*Knocks at the door.*

Mrs Truf. (*At the window.*) Who's there?

Truf. Who else my jewel but your own deer Trushoop? open the dure if you plaze my jewel

Mrs. Truf. Not I, by my confhence !—go back to the hoeres where you cum from. I'll not be difturbed by you this way fo I won't.

Truf. Open the dure, my deer if you plaze, the nabours will make a grate tawk if you wou'd, for nabour ghibungs people are all up.

Mrs Truf. What do I care for the nabours, they know I'm an honeft vartuous woman, an that's more than they can fay of you, an it's no matter how foon they know of your goings on, if you ftay out every night in the morning.

Truf. Well if you won't open it yourfelf my fwateft, why then call Tarrance, if you plaze.

Mrs Truf. Indeed, an indeed an I'll call no Tarrance, if you want Tarrance, why then call him yourfelf, I'll no' be ftaying up in the cowl, killing my life this way fo I won't.

[*She retires from the window.*

Truf. (*Knocks at the door*) Tarrance !—Tarrance !—Tarrance !

Tar. (*Anfwers within*) Cumming Sir

Truf. Well then come away, an faith ! I an you will go to work togeder, fo we will, for by my fowl the fhap will be the fillefht place in the houfe for me, for by St. Patrick, an I'd rather hear the Coopers march, than the found of my wife's tung the day. (*Knocks again*) Tarrance !—Tarrance !—

Tar. (*Within*) Cumming.

Truf. Augh ! this oath—this day will be a bad night to me—Well the devil a hare I care—when I get the money fhe'll foon make it up wid me—faith I'll make her as grate as the Arle of Portledown's own wife—Lady Barrymore fhan't be finer than fhe ! (*He knocks and calls Tarrance*) why you tief of the wurld ! if you don't cum down in a minute, I'll give you fhelaley !—why Tarrance !

Tar. (*Within*) I'm juft here

Truf. This fellow's enough to wurry the pafhence of St. Ignatius, or the holy Pope himfelf. Tarrance !—you devil you !

Tar (*Opens the door*) Shure I am juft here.

Truf. You tief of the wurld, what made you let me in when I tumpt ?

Tar. Shure I cumm'd when I heard you cawl—

Truf. You lie you tief !

Tar (*Scratching his head and grumbling*) Shure if you cumm'd home in time we wouldn't have all this bodtheration, so we wouldn't.

Truf. Give us none of your gum vea fonslpere of perdition —by my foul an I'll give you Shelaley. (*He beats him.*)

Tar. (*Bawls out aloud*) O murder!—murder! master deer lave off, don't kill one.

Mrs. Truf. (*Returns to the window.*) Ain't you ashamed to be making a grate noise in the Alley this morning, killing the poor boy for nothing?

Tar. Arra mistress, dare speak till him—master dare lave off, for share I was asleep when I heard you cawl.

Truf. (*Pushing Tarrance from him*) To the devil I pitch all liars—go to your work you tief of the wurld, and if you don't make me five tight keggs the day (that will howld no water) I'll bate you as long as I am able and longer too. (*They cross the alley to the shop.*) [*Exeunt.*

SCENE III. *A Room in M. Placket's house.*

(*Enter* RACCOON *with a Spit, Pick-axe and Spade shouldered.*)

Rac. What shall I do wid dese tings?—dad I'll put dem under de bed [*He steps into the next room puts them under the bed and returns.*] But where's Mrs. Placket?—she'll be oberjoyed when I tell her,—dad I'll dress her off as fine as de Queen of Shebas, when she come to see brudder Solomon—she shall go to de plays every night, wid a coach and two footmen to tend her [*He calls*] Placket! Pet! Pet!

Plack. (*Within*) Pets a coming—Pets a coming, dear Cooney.

(*Enter* PLACKET.)

Rac. Buss me my dear, and I'll tell you someting, dat will make you happy.

Plack. What! is your wife dead? say—tell me—for I know that will make us both happy!

Rac. No, no—but its bery near so good—but you'll tell—

Plack. No, indeed, indeed and double deed—I won't my dear Cooney.

Rac. Well den—I'll not keep my dear Pet in suspense any longer—but you must buss me, when I say any ting dat pleases you.

Plack. Well! so I will, a hundred and a hundred times.

Rac. Well den—but you'll tell? If you do I'll neber forgib you.

Plack. Trust me dear Cooney—did I ever betray any of your secrets?

Rac. Why no pet—den I'll tell you. Mr. Hurt has receeb'd a letter from his sister in law in England wid an account of two or tree hunder'd tousand pound, and some oder tings, dat was buried by old Blackbeard de pirate wid de draft where it is hid, and we know de berry spot—(*she kisses him*) and I'll gib you five hunderd a year for pin money (*kisses*) and we'll ride in de coach togedder (*kisses*) and we'll go to de play togedder (*kisses*) and den we'll come home and go to bed togedder (*kisses*) and den we'll—a you little rogue you, (*kisses again.*)

Plack. And do you really think you'll find it?

Rac. Why yes, to be sure child—we know de berry spot!

Plack. Why if you knew where all the treasure in the world was buried, you'd never obtain it without a conjuror.

Rac. Yes my dear, but we hab a conjuror, weeb got Mr. Rattletrap, he understands astrology and de magic art, better den Doctor Foster or any man in de gubberment, and dis night we intend to make de trial,—and I must go dis instant and settle de place of meeting.

Plack. And can you leave me so soon, my dear Cooney?

[RACCOON *sings.*]

SONG VI.

O! how joyful shall I be,
When I get de money,
I will bring it all to dee;
O! my diddling honey. [*Exit singing.*

Plack. Bye bye Cooney. Good luck attend him, for my sake. Poor old fool! he thinks I have a prodigious fondness for him, and so I have for his better part—that's his money. He has been deficient in payment for some time past, and now tells me a cock and a bull story of hidden treasure, to amuse and deceive me—accompanied with a delire of soft slobbering language, such as, his pet, his dove, his poor ting, and a thousand such childish expressions and things I'm up with him,—for I call him Cooney, cock-a-pidgeon, sugar plumb, cock a dandy, and all the sweet things I can think of, and was any one to overhear us, they would think us two little children playing baby, and really we do little more. But thank fortune! I'm not at a loss for a friend to make up his deficiency, tho' he thinks me as innocent as a dove; and indeed I'm like a dove, in one respect, for when I lose one mate, I mourn till I get another—but I hope the worst is past.

SONG VII.

Tho' I hate the old wretch, full as bad as Jack Ketch,
My necessities tell me to please him,
I will ogle and whine, till I make the gold mine;
For that's the best method to ease him.
I'll simper and leer, and I'll call him my dear,
And be loving as ever I can be,
Then hasten dear Cooney, and fetch me the money;
For that will exact to my plan be. (*Exit singing.*

SCENE IV. *A Street.*

(*Enter* QUADRANT *and* HUM, *meeting* RATTLETRAP.)

Hum. Hey! Rattletrap, which way?

Rat. I've just return'd from the place of action. We go on gloriously! Quadrant and I must set out half an hour before the rest, to have all things in readiness—I've left Spitfire here and given him his proper cue.

Hum. Very good! What do you think? Ha! ha! I just now saw brother Raccoon, with a long catalogue of all his military achievements both in Jamaica and on the Continent, together with a Treatise he wrote on Tactics, last war, for the instruction not only of our militia, but the regular officers likewise. The same he exhibited in the Coffee-house—you remember it—I could scarcely refrain from laughing, while he was so earnest in explaining to me de hollow square, and de ebolutions, as he call'd 'em. He's gone in great haste, to lay 'em before the Governor, to procure his recommendation to the Secretary at War, for a Kurnell's Commission, as he term'd it. I find nothing less than a Regiment will satisfy him, which, he thinks his transcendent ment alone entitles him to: but whether or not, he swears he'll make his gold subservient to his ambition, when he obtains it.

Quid. Ha! ha! I believe he will truly, when he obtains it. Ha! ha! ha!

Hon. I'm at a loss to guess how he'll bear up, under his disappointment. Nothing can equal his folly but his vanity.—But I have hopes this experiment, in company, will cure him.

R t. No matter how much he's disappointed. I'm doubtful, persons of his turn, are incapable of proper reflection.

Hon. True—but its a great pity for all.—Well, remember we're all to meet at the Tun, precisely at six. (*Takes at his watch.*) We've but half an hour to spare. Adieu! Adieu!

[*Exeunt different ways.*

SCENE V. *A Taylor's shop.*

(*Taylors at work, some singing, others whistling, &c.*)
(*Enter* BUCKRAM, *with his broad sword.*)

Buck. Awa! awa! wi' ye a, awa, begane ye skoondrels, oot o me hoose this meneete, or by St. Andra, Ize chap aff the heeds o every vullain o ye! oot ye vile scum, ra gabble oot o yer heeds or Ize mak a sacrafeeze o ye a. (*He makes a few flourishes with his sword, and cuts off the brass knob of the door. The Taylors all jump off the shop board in confusion, tumbling over each other to the their stockings about their heels, &c. and exit.*) Na mare me hoose sal be a resaptacle for thieves, ye preeklooze cabbaging sins o hoores—thir thirteen years Ize been a servant to ye a—Awa! awa Stay tape, Bockrum, Moohare, Guze, Clips an a. (*He kicks and throws them with remnants, skirts of cloth, and old clothes about the stage.*) Na mare casion ha I for ye, noo Ize clared the shap boord, the next thing is to clare the hall o its rubbage. (*He kicks the scraps, old rags, &c. about from under the shop-board.*) Ize fut up this room for the reception o Congress and gentlemen o the foorst rank,—then Ize gang till Bretain and buy a title, it sal be naething less than Laird Chaumberlain, foorst Laird o the bed chaumber, or meester o the wardrobe, then Ize be e gane freea till America, an noo Ize cased me mine o the parplaxity o buzness,—noo for the gowd,—Ize gang and meet my company.

[*Exit.*

SONG VIII

Ize [illegible] [illegible] po[illegible] c[illegible] clath,
  To [illegible] in [illegible] the [illegible]ate,
[illegible] [illegible] [illegible] [illegible]amb[illegible]e bath
  C[illegible]mbine to mak me grate.
I [illegible] meel [illegible] a place at court,
  Tha[illegible] be[illegible] grandeur suits,
[illegible] scorne [illegible] o the mea[illegible]er sort,
  Lea[illegible] si[illegible]ly paultry brutes.
Oh [illegible] the gowd, the bonny bonny gowd,
  Tha[illegible]s buried near the mull,
Oh! could I get [illegible]e grip o thee
  Then I should ha me wull. [Exit.

SCENE V. *A Room in Washball's house.*

(Enter MEANWELL *and* LUCY*.)*

Mean. I can't co[illegible] my dear Lucy, the mea[illegible] of your uncle's displea[illegible] [illegible] his churlish beha[illegible]our for some days past, gi[illegible]es me great concern.

Lucy. He never [illegible] a [illegible]abl[illegible] to your [illegible] [illegible] [illegible] [illegible] these three days, during which [illegible] he has b[illegible] [illegible] dinning in m[illegible] ea[illegible] that provided I marry agr[illegible], to [illegible] w[illegible]ll red[illegible] give me ten thousand pounds for a [illegible] and [illegible], [illegible] d[illegible] [illegible] if ever I [illegible] to [illegible] [illegible] your [illegible], [illegible] [illegible] me.

Mean. Strange!—but where[illegible] he [illegible] [illegible] [illegible] [illegible]?

Lucy. The Lord knows [illegible] [illegible] certainly [illegible] himself [illegible] [illegible] [illegible] [illegible] [illegible] [illegible]erous [illegible] [illegible] [illegible] he intended [illegible] to sail for [illegible] and there [illegible] [illegible] [illegible] a [illegible] of the Golden fleece.

Mean. [illegible] he must be out of his [illegible], [illegible] never [illegible] talk so inconsistently [illegible] and [illegible] [illegible] for the celebration of our nuptials [illegible] preparations [illegible] of a sudden change his mind!—I cannot account for it.

Lucy. I hope [illegible] [illegible] will shortly change, then we shall bring matters to a conclusion; for it would [illegible] much more agreeable to me, [illegible] than without his final consent.

Mean. Certainly! it would be [illegible] us both; but further con-[illegible], it must be done!

Lucy. Our affair is now carried on too far for us to retract, without subjecting ourselves to the ridicule of the whole town; besides, my dear Meanwell, you know a girl's character, under these circumstances, seldom escapes censure.

Mean. True my dear Lucy! the world's very censorious and slander (like a snow ball) always gathers by rolling; whatever malice can invent, or envy suggest, shall never lessen you in my esteem. I know your virtue and you know my honor! my love to you is of the most pure and evangelical kind! it runs spontaneously into my veins, like a "fountain of living water!" 'Tis fixed irrevocably firm as a rock, impossible to be shaken, by the blasts of an universe of scandalous tongues!

Lucy. Be assured my dearest Meanwell, your generous love, shall be repaid with virtue, tenderness, respect, and obedience; and could I possess the Ten thousand pounds my uncle has swallowed out for me, I should esteem it as so much dross — 'twould only serve to accelerate my misery without you!

SONG IX.

Mean. My dear Lucy you ravish my heart,
I am blest with such language as this;
To my arms then O come! we'll never part,
And now mutually seal with a kiss. (*Kisses.*)

Lucy. Ten thousand sweet kisses I'll give,
O! be you but contented with me,
Then for you my dear Meanwell I'll live;
And as happy as constant I'll be.

Lord! here's my uncle!

(*Enter* WASHBALL.)

Wash. Hey day! here's fine doings indeed! you're a fine young master, are you? how dare you enter my house, after I forbid you?—Eigh sirrah?

Mean. Sir, your niece—and——

Wash. And what?—sirrah!—what have you to do with my niece? out of my house, with your [illegible]; you're a pretty fellow truly! to marry a girl of ten thousand pounds fortune, eigh! [illegible]—I suppose you intend to feed her with wind and [illegible] a family of [illegible] eigh! an't you [illegible]?

Mean. Sir, I beg——

Wash. Beg, why?—I suffer no beggars in my house—begone you rascal!—get out of my house I say—what do you want to rob me, and debauch my niece? eigh! out of my house or I'll break your head, sirrah!

Lucy. Dear uncle, be patient!

Wash. Patient eigh? what, you want me to stay, do you? hussey, get to your room! to your room this instant! (*He attempts to strike her with his cane, Meanwell interposes and receives the blow.*) Get out of my house, you rascal!—away to your room baggage!—out of my house villain!

[*Exit Meanwell and Lucy different ways.*

Wash. (*Out of breath.*) If ever I find you here again you [illegible] dog you, I'll send you to the work house, sirrah! ten thousand pounds cash! to an upstart coxcomb, who has not so much as a coat of arms. Meanwell! mean enough God knows! I'm sure, there's no such name to be found, in all the books of heraldry,—no, no! I'll match my niece to a nobleman who can trace his genealogy as far back, as Edward the Confessor, William the Conqueror, Charles the Fat, or Pope Gregory, Hildebrand, and settle a good jointure on her equal to that I intend to give her. I'll away to Spain and get myself created a knight of the Golden Fleece! then, I shall have a greater coat of arms, than any peer of Great Britain! I shall be then called Mr. Sir John Washball Esquire, Knight of the most noble order of the Golden-Fleece! and then I'll seek out for some handsome noble-blooded young virgin (if I can find one of that character, among that class of people, which I am a little doubtful of these fornicating times) with whom I'll light the hymeneal torch at the connubial altar—tho' I've past my octogenary years of age! what of that? Abra'm, Isaac, and Jacob, were forty times older than I and begat Sons and daughters innumerable and so may I, I' nothing like trying—Oh! how I exult in the prospect but stop, let me see, what if some young cicisbeo, should Crim. Con. me? eigh! egad I shou'dn't like that very well, but then, if he found, I shall have some comfort in knowing I can [illegible] and [illegible] I must [illegible] these [illegible] [illegible] now-a-days [illegible] be among the great [illegible] [illegible] [illegible], [illegible] may as well be [illegible] of [illegible] world [illegible] H[illegible], [illegible] I'll [illegible] [illegible] and [illegible] the [illegible], the [illegible] diamond's and rubies, that make the [illegible], [illegible] mould [illegible], when lodg'd in the mine, [illegible] but [illegible] wanting

> Which now lie dormant, in our mother earth,
> But [illegible] labour hard, [illegible]
> For money I'll have and I am resolv'd to [illegible],
> My fate, [illegible] the adventure die! [*Exit*

ACT II. *SCENE I.*

(*Scene opens and discovers Mrs. Trowel at work in her parlour.*)

(*A knocking at the door.*)

Mrs Trow. Who's there? walk in.

(*Enter Mrs. Trusty.*)

Mrs Trus. An how are you Mrs. Trowell?

Mrs Trow. Oh! [illegible], dear Mrs. Trusthope, I [illegible] to see you, take a chair. I make bold to request the favour of your good company to take a dish of tea; you are become a great stranger of late.

Mrs Trus. Indeed an indeed the whole world and every thing in it seems strange to me of late—all going to destruction.

Mrs. Trow. Lord! how?—tell me—I have been very uneasy for some time past, thinking I might have unknowingly offended you. God knows my heart! we used to be as intimate as two lovers, and nothing would give me half so much pleasure as a continuance of our old sweet intimacy.

Mrs Trus. Augh! an its all over with the like of that now.

Mrs. Trow. The like of what? speak plain, have I offended you?

Mrs. Truf. No, indeed an you haven't.

Mrs Trow. Then why do you absent yourself and look so dejected of late? what is the matter—tell me, do!

Mrs. Truf. Matter enough God knows!

Mrs Trow You aston sh me!—you know I'm your friend, hide nothing from me it may be I can serve you

Mrs Trus Impossible! say no more about it, I know your goodness (*Cries*) What did this carpet cost you?

Mrs Trow Pshaw! fifteen pounds—but pray tell me?

Mrs. Trus My worthless husband promis'd me one long ago but poor dear I am [illegible] to be able to buy a house cloth to wipe the [illegible] (*Cries*)

Mrs Trow O! tell me what's the matter, I vow my heart bleeds for you

Mrs Trus I can't

Mrs Trow You can

Mrs Trus I must not.

Mrs Trow You must, you shall.

Mrs Trus No never.

Mrs Trow I insist upon it! remember the many hours we and our husbands have passed together, in social mirth and conversation in visiting in card parties in going to plays in sleighing, and in tripping to Gray's Gardens, they calling each other Brother, on account of their being Free masons, and we in consequence of it calling each other sister

Mrs Trus Curse the name! that I fear is the source of all my sorrows.

Mrs Trow. What name, Sister?

Mrs Trus No, indeed

Mrs Trow Brother.

Mrs Trus No

Mrs Trow What then pray?

Mrs Trus Free mason (*Cries*)

Mrs Trow Gracious goodness!—how?

Mrs. Trus Why now Mrs Trowell, you force me to spake, when I don't want to spake Why, Trushoop (an I'll say that for him) ever since we were man and wife, which is now two and twenty years, twelve months, an I think, thirty four days, kept good hours, till he got into that cursed club of Free masons an they have been the ruin of him, sowl an body! an my own self an family in the bargain, an we shall all in a little time be beggars!

Mrs. Trow. I hope not! Lord don't say so! quite opposite

[illegible] les [illegible] you are [illegible] Mrs Trus-loop

Mrs Trus Profess!—[illegible]

Mrs Trow. Why, then [illegible] are Chastity, [illegible] and Charity [illegible]

Mrs Trus Hypocrite, [illegible] (C[illegible] her

Mrs Trow O fye! O [illegible]! [illegible] how?

Mrs Trus Why, do [illegible] Trusloop [illegible] company [illegible] lodge, [illegible] him away [illegible] house [illegible] staying out all night [illegible] morning, [illegible] all the neighbours [illegible] many [illegible] many a times [illegible] now, [illegible]?

Mrs Trow I have [illegible], but [illegible] the [illegible] reflections cast on [illegible] They are [illegible] virtuous gentlemen, [illegible] acquainted [illegible] philosophy, Architecture, Morality, [illegible]

Mrs Trus [illegible] indeed—[illegible] you [illegible] better [illegible] that Mrs Trowell

Mrs Trow I know [illegible] my husband has been a Free [illegible] goes to church more frequently than he [illegible] every night and morning [illegible] before and after meals

Mrs Trus A [illegible] nation, [illegible] The devil [illegible] But [illegible] often heard your man or God [illegible] your own [illegible] various unseasonable hours.

Mrs Trow I [illegible] Mrs Trusloop but [illegible] Free masons are not to blame

Mrs. Trus By my conscience! but they are [illegible] Trusloop [illegible] your saint [illegible] goes together [illegible] The devil [illegible] barrel the better [illegible]—I wonder now [illegible] how you can be so [illegible], Mrs Trowell?

Mrs Trow. When I married first, I was for some time very uneaſ[illegible] [illegible] our like ourſelf; but I have learned patience and reſignation, and conſidering that my huſband continued to go to church and ſay his prayers and graces as uſual—I thought that poſſibly, I might be jealous without ſufficient cauſe.

Mrs Truſ. Sure [illegible] as he dont pray at night only to be let in, in the morning, pon my ſowl! now Mrs Trowell, as you may talk and talk till your as black as your [illegible] about his going to church an prayers, an graces, an [illegible] and patience—I tell you now, and so I do—why now, and do you not read of the [illegible] in the goſpel how he opened his windows to let the people ſee him pray? and he was as great a raſcal as ever tread ſhoe leather, an a free-maſon too, I warrant the [illegible]—but I won't be put off ſo—ſo I wouldn't.

Mrs Trow. Lord! how you talk! Mrs ——

Mrs Truſ. Lawk! are faith an I towld Truſhoop t'oder day, I would know the truth—I [illegible] with him ſo I did,—I [illegible] him—I expoſtulated with him again an again—I raved—I raged—I ſtamped—I ſtormed—I vow'd—I proteſted—I ſwore (an faith I curſt him! God forgive me for curſing a brute baaſt,) that he ſhould never put his futt in bed with me, (an God forgive me for [illegible] ſuch a rash oath) till he towld me the razon of his kaping ſuch bad hours—an don't you think it, Mrs. Trowell? the [illegible] word I got out of him, at all at all—an he went over to the ſhop, and I went after, and I razoned again an again with him till my poor hart was next dure to burſting,—an he bate the koopers mallet on the barrel, an made ſuch a confounded noiſe all the time, he wouldn't hare me ſpake a word, at all at all—ſo I was deviliſh mad that I bate him with the tick end of the hoop pole about every turn.—ſo I wou'dn't give him a toot full to ate, an a poor devil he has been ſtarving for this week to cum, an by [illegible], [illegible] he ſhall have none from me, ſo he ſhall—let him go eat with the hoores where he cum from.

Mrs Trow. O! gracious!—if ever I heard the like!—you cruel creature!—how could you ſerve him ſo?

Mrs Truſ. Cruel!—faith! an he ought to be ſent to the Baltic, an Button, bay in the bargin.

Mrs Trow. Merciful father, how you talk!

Mrs Trus. Hawk indeed!

Mrs Trow. Well, thank God! I took a contrary method with my husband, and have succeeded to the utmost of my wishes having thereby discovered the mystery.

Mrs Trus. An what mistery? pray now?

Mrs Trow. So don't fret your husband nor make yourself uneasy any more, take my word for it, it will a'l——[*coughs.*]

Mrs Trus. All what pray now?

Mrs Trow. Turn out for the better.

Mrs Trus. O alas! better! an better may be it would, if they would leave off hooting

Mrs Trow. Let 'em alone—let 'em go on in their own way.

Mrs Trus. Go on their own way! may go thence to destruction! spending their time, health and substance! do you call that turn out for the better? Lord! how you tawk!—I'm ashamed of you indeed an I am Mrs Trowell—you're strangely altered to what you was

Mrs Trow. No, no, that is not the case nor consequence

Mrs Trus. I am shure but it is—shure an your out of your senses

Mrs Trow. No God forbid

Mrs Trus. You must be near it.

Mrs. Trow. I am not.

Mrs Trus. Fat then are you, else what do you mane by your misteries—and all for the better—fath and it was misterious sort of tawk so it is

Mrs Trow. Come, come, don't be angry—I'll tell you, and you'll be as well pleased with the happy discovery as I was, after undergoing much anxiety from it; and knowing the soft and loving temper of my husband, I wheedled, I coax'd, I fondled, I hugged, I squeezed, I caressed and I kissed him till I got the whole secret out of him; so I confess, in some degree, I was obliged to act the Delilah, for you know a man of feeling and sensibility, cannot long withstand the solicitations of a woman he loves; they are all Sampsons, I assure you. In short, he unbosomed his whole mind to me, and if I had been so minded, I could have got the whole secret of free masonry out of him, but I despifed taking that advantage of him, knowing he must have perjur'd himself.

Mrs. Truf. An what is it? pray let's hear you've been a long time about it.

Mrs. Trow. Have a little patience and I heartily congratulate you on our pleasing prospect of flowing in wealth, and notwithstanding your forbodings of poverty it will turn out the happiest circumstance of our lives enable us to live, not only independent but in a superlative station.

Mrs. Truf. My God! arn't you humbugging me now? Mrs. Trowell.

Mrs. Trow. No indeed, I'm not capable of it.

Mrs. Truf. An can you be serious?

Mrs. Trow. I am upon honour.

Mrs. Truf. An how is this miracle to be regl.t? Oh! I shall faint.

Mrs. Trow. Pshaw! never faint at good news—don't be so weak Mrs. Trufhoop, keep a steady even temper. [*She brings a small bottle of cordial and a glass.*] Drink a little of this. [*She drinks.*] I hope you feel more compos'd Mrs. Trufhoop?

Mrs. Truf. Troth hon I'ale a good dale better—go give me another glass Mrs. Trowell, that will compose me. [*Gives her another glass.*] Augh! an I'm bravely now. But, pray go on, where you laft off—don't kape me so long, or else I shall faint again.

Mrs. Trow. Refume your former chearfulness—banish jealousy and suspicion—keep your fairit up. "Be not faithless, but believe." Well, now I'll tell you. Mr. Hum and Mr. Quadrant, both Free masons, have a certain knowledge of a vast sum of money, and rich jewels that was formerly hid by the pirates, and they meet every night at the Tun to consult together and prepare themselves, to go one of these nights to dig it up—out of brotherly love to my husband and yours, and two or tree others, have communicated the secret in confidence to them, and they are to come in for equal shares, and this accounts for their staying out so late—the Tun is the bawdy-house they frequent, and now I hope Mrs. Trufhoop, you will make yourself easy, and treat your husband with more humanity and kindness,

Mrs. Truf. Troth! an I will—if its trute—but how will they find the plashe?

Mrs. Trow. Why bless you!—by the virtue and power of masonry, and the knowledge of Mr. Rattletrap, the conjurer; and they have got magic lanthorns, dark-lanthorns, spy-glasses, telescopes, compasses, quadrants, spades, shovels, boring-augers, spits, and other implements, in great forwardness

Mrs. Truf. Good luck to 'em, an' blassings on masons and masonary: an ten-thousand blassings on Rattletrap Oh! my dare Trufhoop, how ill I have trated you, my hart is vary sorry for it, but poor fowl! I'll come and make it up with you. *(Rises.)*

Mrs Trow O no! not yet!—you shall stay tea first.

Mrs Truf Not I, by my conshence, do you think now an I can sit azey here, an see him, poor fowl! starving at home!—not I indeed! I never cou'd, Mrs. Trowell *(Going.)*

Mrs Trow Psha!—what nonsense! stay, do—tea is nearly ready.

Mrs Truf No, indeed! an indeed! an I cannot. I'll go this instant, and make him a good dish of grane-tay at home, for poor fowl! he is starv'd to death already, and he may die with starvation, or the hyperphobe, for he s ate nutting but vater in my houshe for this two weeks to come, so he has. *(Going.)*

Mrs Trow. Poh! poh! what nonsense—do stay.

Mrs Truf Not for the wurld! how hard-harted you are now.

Mrs Trow. You're always on the extremes—I'll send for him to drink tea with us.

Mrs Truf No, No!—I want a little private tawk with him, I'll cum again to-morrow—Good bye, good bye

Mrs Trow. Well, see you do. Good bye *(Exit Mrs. Trufhoop.)* An unsteady woman! soon rais'd and soon depress'd. But I was short, I didn't caution her against giving any cause of suspicion of what is going on I fear, she by her indiscretion may ruin the project, by blabbing it out, among the neighbours in the alley, who are not very remarkable for taciturnity, any more than herself,—it would be a fatal discovery, and the blame all fall upon me —I must see her directly, and settle that point. [*Exit.*

SCENE II *Scene opens and discovers* RATTLETRAP, HUM, QUADRANT, RACCOON, BUCKRAM, TRUSHOOP, WASHBALL, *and* TROWELL, *seated round a table, with wine, &c.*

(*Enter* PARCHMENT)

Parch My old friend, Mr Trushoop, how are you?

Trus O hone a cree! O! my deer, at your sarvish—but I don't care how I am—so you are well (*Shakes hands.*

Parch. Hah! hah!—I hope you're all well, gentlemen.

Trow Come, Mr Parchment, sit down.

Hum. Are we all here, gentlemen?

Trus Troth! an here's the hole-tote of us, burds of a fedder flock togedder.

Hum Then we'll proceed to business:—Well, gentlemen, every thing seems to go on prosperously, and bear a favourable aspect—I think my-myself happy, in not having disclosed this important secret, to any of the vain or profligate part of mankind—but to you, gentlemen, who, by a long series of acquaintance, I've found to be men of the strictest honor and integrity, which leaves me no room to doubt, but that the treasure, we're now about to discover and divide amongst us, will be so disposed of, as to render each of us useful members of society, and shining ornaments to the government under which we live —It would grieve my heart to see any of you act inconsistent with the character of a man of piety and a gentleman!

Trus. Arra! my deer, that's true for you! *(Aside.)* Don't you see, that vary fine spache he made just now?—by my sowl! an he's a jintelman of grate larnedness! fath! an he is. I'll warrant him now, an he's got Egypt's fables all by heart, so he has.

Qual. *(Aside.)* He is certainly a man of great cognascence.

Trus. *(Aside.)* No sense?—fath! an he's got forty times more sense than you honey.

Low. *(Aside.)* Hah!—hah! what a queer dog!

Rac. We tank brudder Hum, for his kind admonitions, what he says is trute, and springs from de berry fountain of [illegible], and as my [illegible] lie in de militar[illegible]; I intend to buy de reg'ment—den I'll show dem, what de 'mericans can do, *([illegible] the [illegible] of [illegible] with his cane.)* "Safe bind, safe find!"—ha! brudder Hum?—I hab engag'd wid Mr. Treppick, and hab it from under his own hand, for a bill of exchange for ten thousand pound at sixty-five, at de rate of twenty-eight shilling de pistole, and gold dust at six pound de ounce.

Hum. It's very commendable, brother Raccoon, you have, to be sure, an excellent idea of honour and trade.

Rac. And beside all dis brudder Hum—I will build at my own expence, a comfitable hospital, fo de reception of de poor penitent female prostitutes—obersee dem myself, take care of de poor tings, and dey shall hab all I can gib dem.

Hum. *(Aside.)* What a libidinous old dog!—No doubt of it, brother Raccoon, it's highly meritorious! none so fit to endow and superintend so heaven-born an institution! as yourself; even Solomon, in all his glory

—with all his wisdom and experience in these matters, will be eclipsed by you;—excuse me, brother Raccoon, I almost envy your happiness!—What Bashaw! Grand Signior! or Sultan! will be equal to you?—or what Seraglio on earth, comparable to yours?—It will be a Paradise in reality, and in perfection! far exceeding the imaginary paradise of Mahomet! Oh! happy, happy man! But as I wou'd by no means, presume to direct one so well qualified and conversant in these delicate effeminate matters—yet, methinks, brother Raccoon, were you also to erect a foundling hospital, it would reflect additional lustre on your charity, fame, honor, and glory!

Rac. No, no! brudder Hum—I tink I hab done enough,—let Mr Washball do dat

Wash. No, no! I won't—I'll maintain no body's bastards but my own,—every body would laugh at me, and call me an old fool!—I'll not be pester'd with your brats, I warrant you!—I am far advanc'd in years, and have lost that sprightliness and activity, I possest in my youthful days.

Trou. No doubt of it, Mr. Washball, but you carry your age well.

Buck. Troth! an he does mon.

Wash Aye, aye!—no matter—but I hope to do some good with my money too, I purpose to go to Spain—get myself made a Knight of the Golden-fleece—then to London, and marry my niece to a nobleman—I've no ambition, not I, but to be call'd Mr Sir John Washball, Esq and have a coat of arms

Tru. A night of the whipping-post, you mane—well, the devil a hare myself cares for a cote of arms, or, a co of legs—by my sowl! but I'll buy myself a good pa r vusted stockings, tin'd wid si k one , and myself will bild a chappel, and help the poor pre ests, who havn't a tootful to put in their mouths.—Augh! how I would like to see the poor French emigrants bawling at me?—"Charité pour l'amour de Dieu!" An the devil a baggar shall leave my howshe, widout a hungry bally! let me alone for that! And when I would be after dying,—surely they'll call me Shaint Patrick, junior, and long life to you honey!

Hum. I ap, laud your pious resolutions. Mr Trusshoop, your intentional charity and glorious designs, are certainly disinterested, and worthy of none but yourself!

Tru. The devil a word a lie in all that!

Tare. History cannot produce men of more liberal, generous, philanthropic, humane, christian, charitable, and patriotic sentiments, so truly characteristic of yourselves! Your names, gentlemen, will be handed down with eclat, to the remotest periods of eternity!—Temples—monuments—pillars—obelisks—statues—spires—bustos—and triumphal arches, will rise spontaneously over each of your graves, like so many phoenixes out of their own ashes, and defy the efforts of envy or malice to destroy them!—Nay, should even the old gentleman, Time himself, that pertinacious destroyer of bodies attempt it, he would find himself (perhaps, for the first time) woefully disappointed.

Truf. And a' faith! would he—that's true for you!

Hum. Depend upon it—volumes will swell in your praise—and I myself, (though vastly inferior to the task) will write an encomiastic on each of you, and have them printed in a folio-volume, neatly bound, gilt, and lettered, as large as a church bible.

Rac. Do so, brudder Hum, we tank you for your kind intention.

Truf. None of that, faith! an I wou'dn't suffer Goliah, nor Phin M'Cool himse'f, to comb my head wid a stick!

Quad. (*Aside.*) He! he! he! Surely you won't refuse the honor, Mr. Trushoop?

Trus. Fath! an there s no honor thereabouts, honey!

Parch. (*aside.*) Hah! hah! hah! su prising y humorous.

Quad. (*Aside.*) He is so excessively witty and comical, tis almost impossible to do any business where he is.

Rac. Well, gentlemen,—have you seriously considered what you're going about?—Our warfare is not with the men of this world, we have to engage with principalities and powers of darkness, with invisibles, demons, and hobgoblins, far more powerful than the united legions of the most invincible monarchs on earth: therefore, the utmost exertion of your courage and every nerve, will be absolutely and indispensibly necessary.

Parch. The thoughts of those infernals shocks me so, I can scarcely help trembling!

Rac. I tink I hab courage enough!——

Hawk. Not the least shadow of a doubt, brother Raccoon, you have ever been super-eminently distinguished for your superior courage and military skill!

Quad. Aye, aye, you're a happy man! your courage is constitutional!

Wisp. So it is—so it is—but for me—Oh dear! oh dear!

Rac. Hoot, mon! awa, awa! wi' a yere yealping, na mare o yere [illegible]! (*Sings.*)

SONG X.

Tis money macks the coward brave,
An freedom gies to ev'ry slave,
[illegible] bluid-[illegible], Ize soon displa',
[illegible] *Atarie*, &c.

Stan' ye a ſtill an ſee how tight,
A Scotchman we the deel wull fight,
Ize toozle him e'en at my eaſe;
Drive imps and warlocks down the braes.
Drive imps, &c.

My life Ize lay to a Scotch bawbee,
Ize grup him fauſt ye ſoon ſal ſee,
Rare ſport, my lads, troth! ſoon Ize ſhow,
What a bonny highland lad can do!
What a bonny, &c.

Be he the deel, or what he wu l,
By Andra's-ſaint! he'll ha his full,
Quick 'boot his heed, my ſword ſhall pla',
Mak 'im quut his legs, an' gang awa.
Mak 'im quut, &c.

Waſh. Excellent indeed! that ſong has inſpired me with a little courage.

Hum. I'm glad to hear it! I hope it will inſpire us all, and have the ſame effect as the Marſellois'-hymn!

Rat. Well, are you all furniſhed with tools?

Rac. I provide de pick-axe, de ſpade, and de ſpit,—I left dem wid a friend, but I can ſoon get dem.

Rat. Now, gentlemen, let's fix on a watch-word, whereby we may know each other in the dark.

Parch. Right, Sir! the papers inform us, the treaſure was carried up the creek, on board a canoe.

Waſh. A very good watch-word! Mr. Parchment.

Parch. Then let it be canoe! as it has a reference to the concealment of the treaſure.

Hum. Be it ſo—I like the word well.

Buch. Troth! Ize na objection, ſae we con underſtond ane anither.

Trow. I like the word, it has a ſoft ſound, and readily conveyed.

Truſ. The devil a hair myſalf cares how it is, or what it is, canoe! or bote! ſo we get the money!

SONG XI

By Shain Patrick, deer honey's, no longer let's stay,
But take lave altogather an bundle away,
To the plashe underground, where the trazure's expos'd;
An bring that to light, which sha l ne'er be disclos'd.
An now we have got it, my jewels, ohone!
For kaaping it snug—arra! let me alone!
We'll sing Phillalew! at the sight of the pelf,
An, as to the sharing—lave that to myself.

Arra! fale how I'll work, wid my peck ax an spade,
For sure I was nurs'd to the turf-cutting trade,
In bright Tipperara an smiling Tyrone;
An if you'll all help me, we'll all dig a'one.
Come, come then away, to the plashe we'll retrate,
If the devil shou d mate us, he'd surely get bate,
I'll fassen my leg wid a pare of good brogues;
An I'll follow afore, all the way my sweet rogues.

An now we have got it, we'll roar an we'll bawl,
An sing, faith! like locusts in winter an fall,
With shamrough in hat, deel a down will we lay,
But dance all night long, on St Patrick's day,
The bagpipes shall fidd e Graamudgey gramagh,
While we swill down Skolrankey an good lique ragh,
When I wawk in the strate, I'll be led by a trupe,
Coming after an crying,—"Long life to Trushoop!"

Ham. An excellent song 'pon my soul! well compos'd and well sung!

Quad. And well tim'd too! he! he! he!—Is it one of your own composition, Mr Trushoop?

Trus. Why you devil you!—do you tink now, an I'd sing any body's songs but my own!—by my sowl! now, an I'll challenge the whole college of Dublin it's self, to fellow me the like of it!

Hum, *Quad* and *Patch*. Ha! ha! ha!

Rat. (*Aside.*) Hah! ha! ha!—a queer dog! an eccentric genius!—Well, gentlemen, at eleven o'clock we're to meet at the ſtone-bridge, near the mill;—it will not be prudent to go altogether, leſt we be diſcover'd; whoever arrives there firſt, let him wait for the reſt, and as they approach they muſt hail with the watch-word, canoe!—thoſe within muſt anſwer with the ſame word; by obſerving this, we ſhall prevent miſtakes and diſcovery.

Hum. Aye!—aye! the utmoſt care and circumſpection are neceſſary, we can't be too cautious, the object we are purſuing is equal to one whole year's revenue of the United States!

Truſ. Faith! and I'll hollow canew! an canew! all night long in the morning, if you plaze.

Rat. Unleſs you're determined to follow implicitly my directions, when we come to action, 'twill be in vain to proceed.

Waſh. I'll do nothing but what you order, Mr. Rattletrap, indeed I won't! the ſpirits won't hurt us, I hope?

Rat. Don't be afraid—take no raſh ſteps—follow my directions, and not a hair of your heads ſhall be injured! Now, gentlemen, 'tis time to cloſe, 'tis needleſs to ſay any more, now the plan's ſettled. Remember eleven o'clock, at the ſtone-bridge, each of you repair home, and bring all your tools with you, we'll break up for the preſent, I'll away home, and put on my magic habit—otherwiſe, I ſhall have no power over the inviſible!

Rac. I'll go and get de tools, and bring a little refreſhment wid me.

Truſ. Faith! an I'll fatch my gauging-rod, an all the tools in the ſhop, if you want um, becaze why—I'll have no 'caſion to uze um after this, honey!

Buc. Ize feetch my Andra wi' me, an then Ize fece the deel himsel' agin he appear

Quad. And I'll bring the inftruments with me, they are all in excellent order, and well prepared.

Rat. Now gentlemen, let's go with good hearts, there's nothing like putting a good face on thefe matters. If you'll bear chorus, I'll fing you a fong before we fet off Come, fill your glaffes.

All, fay, With all my heart! [*They fill their glaffes.*

SONG XII

The merchant roams from climes to climes,
  Regardlefs of his pleafure,
To hardfhips and fatigue refigns,
  When in purfuit of treafure.

Chorus—And a digging, &c.

See now the lucky hour it comes,
  With pick-axe and with fpade,
A little digging,—oh! my fons,
  And then our fortune's made! *Chorus.*

Let's boldly venture on the ground!
  And feize the glorious cheft,
No joy on earth like gold is found,
  To eafe the human breaft! *Chorus.*

[*All drink, Huzza, and Exeunt.*

SCENE III. A Room in Trufhoop's Houfe.

(*Enter Mrs.* TRUSHOOP *in hafte.*)

Mrs. Truf. Dolly!—Dolly!—

Dolly. Ma'am!

Mrs. Truf. Come hither, girl!—quick! quick!

Dolly. Coming Ma'am.—(*afide.*) What the deuce is the matter now?—fure the houfe is on fire!

Mrs. Truf. Why Dolly! I fay——

(*Enter* DOLLY *running and looking affrighted.*)

Dolly. Here, ma'am.

Mrs. Truf. How long you ftay, huffey?—a body muft fplit their troats afore you cum—go your ways, an put on the tay-kittel, quick! make hafte girl! do you hare?

Dolly. Yes ma'am—(*Afide.*)—Is that all? [*Exit Dolly.*

Mrs Truf. How fhe ftands?—Gaping—I feem in a flutter—my heart fales as light as a fedder,—I don't know what ales me—poor Trufhoop! an I wonder what he'll think, when I tell him all poor devil! an why didn't he tell me himfelf then? an I fhou'dn't have fcowlded him, an bate him, an ftarved him fo, but fure, an its his own fault, but I'll foon make it up with him, Dolly! I fay.

Dolly Ma'am!

Mrs. Truf Does the kittle bile?—you're a plagey while about it

Dolly Juft now, ma'am. (*Afide.*) Plague on yourfelf! you're in a devil of a hurry, I think!—won't give one time to blow the fire, and juft come from ftuffing herfelf at Mrs Trowell's, and not fatisfied, I'll warrant her, fhe's drank twenty difhes of tea, and eat half a cord of toaft and butter!—I hate fuch gormandizing devils!

Mrs. Truf. It feems ev'ry minnet was an hour with me, I fale vary comical!—well, it will be over bye an bye, an faith! an I'll have a better carpet than Mrs. Trowell's, an all thefe ould fafhion chairs, an tab'es, an luckin-glaffes.—I'll pack to the vandue, an I'll buy good Moll-Hoggeny ones—plate, china, an ev'ry thing alfe, fhall be of the neweft tafte an higheft cut, an why fhou'dn't it? fure an I can afford it now? Augh! an good luck to 'um, I fay —Dolly, now an what are you about?

Dolly Blowing the fire, ma'am. (*Afide.*) What the devil do you think?

Mrs. Truf. Wh now! an how long will you blow it?

Dolly. 'Till it boils, ma'am.—(*Aside.*) To be sure.

Mrs. Trus. Why don't you cum then you pukeing toad you!

Dolly. Coming Ma'am (*aside*) I believe in my soul! she's got the influenza, or the ravenous fever, or something!

Mrs. Trus Well, an that self same Mrs. Trowell, is a Jewel of a woman,—what pashence she has, an I wish I had half so much; but faith! an I never will—An why don't you come, you slomakin, with the tay-kittel? bring it along, I say!

Dolly, Yes, ma'am! I'm coming. (*Aside*) Curse the kettle, it will never boil, I can't make it boil for my sou! smoaking my eyes out, and be bother'd so, I swear! I'll plague myself no longer about it, she shall have it as it is, boil or not boil, the devil a bit I care!

Mrs. Trus. Well cum away then, you pokeing toad you!

Dolly. (*aside.*) O! hold your jaw! you brimstone devil!—Coming ma'am!

(*Enter* DOLLY, *with the tea-kettle*)

Mrs. Trus. An did it bile now?

Dolly. Yes, ma'am, over and over again.

Mrs Trus. Curse you, an what made you so long then?

Dolly. To make it boil well, ma'am.

Mrs Trus. Set it down, how you stand gaping? an go your ways over to the shap, and give my complisance to your master, an tell him to cum over, I want to spake till him immediately, while I make a bowl of punch, your master loves punch, (*Aside*) an faith! an I don't like it very badly nather Pull up, my girl!

Dolly Yes, ma'am. (*Aside*) Hatey titey, and what's all this going on? Some fun, I believe in my soul! Hah! hah! hah!—Oh! goodee, goodee oh! we shall see presently. [*Exit* DOLLY.

Mrs. Truf. Well indeed I an I believe it's true enuff, an I have dram't it, or read it in fome ould alminac fomewhere, that "there is great joy over one finner that rapanteth." Troth! an I'm fhure an I rapant of of ftarving him fo, an poor Trufhoop will have grate joy now, when he knows what I'm going about to do for him, poor fowl! an he muft be vary hungry, fo he muft, not a drop has he ate in my houfhe, this fix days to cum, an indeed, an indeed, he is one of the beft huf-bands I ever fee! [*Exit.*

SCENE IV. A Room in Moll Placket's Houfe

(*Enter* TOPINLIFT, *meeting* MOLL PLACKET.)

Top. What cheer, Moll? let's tafte your head, (*Kiffes her.*) How ftands the wind? is the coaft clear? no danger of the enemy?

Plack. No, no, he has no certain time of coming, except after church on Sundays; and then he never fails, if the old fellow fucceeds in this night's enter-prife, I'll make your fortune for you, my boy!

Top. Why! what the devil has Raccoon fpied now? is there a galloon in chafe? or, is he going to turn pirate?

Plack. No, no, but he may thank the pirates for it!

Top. How, how Moll? tell me, you little dear dog you, (*Chucking her under the chin.*)

Plack. I tell you indeed!—a body wou'd—well, can you keep a fecret then?

Top. Aye! can I, as fnug as a Free-mafon; If ever I blow you, blaft me! you know me better: If one word goes through my head rails, the devil blow me to Halifax, or Botany-Bay.—Aye Moll! the next hur-ricane blow me off the main-top-gallant-yard! three leagues aftern, and be fwallow'd up like Jonathan fwallow'd the whale! That's enough! and now I'll kifs the book on it. (*Kiffes her.*)

Plack. Well, come, I'll tell you—You must know, that Mr Hum has got a letter, and a heap of papers, from his sister-in-law in England, giving an account, where there's a vast deal of money, that was formerly buried by the pirates!

Top. Money! buried by the pirates? the devil!—aye Moll, that's true! I've often heard that Blackbeard hid his money, somewhere by the river's side; but how the devil came she by the papers?

Plack. Why you fool!—she's Captain Blackbeard's great-grand-daughter, and they were preserved in the family till they were sent to Mr Hum, and you know Raccoon is a Free-mason too, so he is to assist him, and they are to go shares.

Top. But how do you know that Hum's a Free-mason?

Plack. Why he told me so, and they always call one another brother, and they keep this business as secret as their masonry, but I wheedled Raccoon out of it, in spite of all his cunning.

Top. By heav'ns! I shou'dn't like him on board the Europa!—he'd make a damn'd fist in the Killecranky trade—he'd throw out a signal, and the custom-house officers wou'd soon bear down on us—away goes ship and cargo by the mast—by the Lord Harry, he'd soon make beggars of my owners—But tell us, Moll, how the devil did you pump it out of him?

Plack. That's none of your business, sauce-box—women like me, have always a lure to catch the men's secrets!

Top. True Moll—but we'll talk further on this subject another time, this sort of chit-chat keeps us at long shot, let's step into the state-room, you know the old saying, "Time and tide waits for no one"

Plack. Softly!—don't be too hasty, let's make the door fast first. (*She locks the door*) Though I love your little finger bette than Raccoon's whole body, yet I must keep in with him.

Top. Aye! that's true Moll—I should be loth to quarrel with an owner, because he did not understand navigation!

Plack. You know he maintains me, (after some sort) finds me a house to live in, fathers all my children, and a husband can do no more.

Top. Right, Moll! now we're all fang, the hatches all secur'd. [*sings.*

SONG XVII.

No girl with Placket can compare,
She is so charming, sweet, and fair,
Such rosy cheeks, and nut-brown hair!
There's none like Molly Placket.

When'ere from sea I do return,
I for my Placket singe and burn,
Good luck, Raccoon, 'tis now my turn,
Come, come my lovely Placket.

Come Moll, now I'll try what the clues of your hammock are made of.

(*As they walk towards the upper part of the stage, a scene opens, and discovers a bed, table, and two bottles on it, with a broken glass over one, and a candle stuck in the other.—A knocking at the door.*)

Top. Zounds! what's this? the devil has ow'd me a spite this long time, and now he has brought the enemy upon me, now I'm land lock'd!

Plack. Who's there?—who's there?

Rac. (*Without.*) It's only me, my liddle dear pet—open de door.

Plack. (*Aside.*) Oh! curse his head!—Pet's a coming! Pet's a coming, dear Cooney!

Top. Where the devil shall I stow myself? by the Lord Harry!—there's no dropping astern here.

Pack Creep under the bed, and your as safe as a thief in a synagogue!

Top. Aye, Moll! down the fore-scuttle, or, any port in a storm, damme!

[*Top. lift goes under the bed, and she opens the door.*

(*Enter* RACCOON.)

Plack What brings my dear Cooney back so soon? no misfortune, I hope

Rac. No, no; no misfortune, only I left sum tings under de bed

Plack. (*Aside.*) Curse your contrivance, now I'm blown What things, my dear Cooney, did you leave there? (*Aside*) Oh! invention! thou darling genius of my sex, assist me, or I'm ruin'd!

Rac. Nutting, my dear pet, but de spade, de pick-axe, and de spit But, what makes you look so supris'd! child?

Plac Why, I was afraid you'd catch me, and indeed you had like to have done so, (*affects a laugh*) He! he! he!

Rac. Seech what? seech how? What de debil do you mean by seech? Dad! I begin to tink it isn't all lies dat I hear about you, Mrs. Placket, tell me this instant who you hab wid you, or I'll shake you like de debil! (*He shakes her, and she bawls.*) What de debil, you tink to impose upon me, wid you he! he! he! I'll know de trute afore I done, hussey!

Plac. Oh! my dear Cooney!—do let me go, and I'll tell you the truth—indeed I will.

Top (*Peeping*) Oh! the brimstone whore!—I wish I was on board the Europa!

Rac Well, come den—confine youself to de trute, hussey!

Top. (*Peeping.*) By the Lord Harry! the storm gathers, we shall have foul weather soon—I must bowse taught my rolling tackles!

Plack. Lord Sir! I'm afraid to tell you—you look so angry—I'll tell you in the morning, when your passion's over.

Rac. I'll know it instantly, you vile strumpet you—or I'll shake you to atoms. (*Shakes her again, and she bawls.*)

Top. (*Peeping.*) It comes thicker and faster,—here's a damn'd stink of bildge water along-side.

Plack. I'll tell you all—if you'll let me go.

Rac. Tell den huffey! dis minnet!

Top. (*Peeping.*) Avast! there—belay that, I must out tomkins, and prepare for a broadside—damme.

Plack. Look at this book. (*Gives him a Dutch almanac.*)

Top. (*Peeping.*) No near! steady there!

Rac. What of dat?—why it's High Dutch.

Plack. Can't you read it?

Rac. No—not I.

Plack. (*Aside.*) I'm glad of it!—Why then, you must know, when I was about fifteen years of age, I lived at Germantown with my uncle, a high German Doctor, who could tell fortunes, find stolen goods, discover hidden treasure, lay spirits, and raise the devil. And his whole art is contained in this little book.

Top. (*Peeping.*) By the Lord! she steers well thro' the breakers, I was dam'd afraid she had sprung a leak, he pump'd her so hellishly!

Rac. You don't say so, pet?

Plack. But I do!—you shall hear—I'd just taken the book in my hand, and raised a familiar spirit, to enquire of him if you'd succeed in your undertaking, and he had just risen thro' the floor, when you knock'd at the door.

Rac. (*Sits and trembles.*) I declare you supprise me! let me get de tings, and I'll go.

Plack. You must not yet, 'tis as much as your life is worth, to touch any thing before I have laid him.

Top. (*Aside.*) By my soul! she acts her part well; she'd out-face truth, and out-brazen the devil! a girl after my own heart, damme.

Rac. Can you lay him den?—my dear pet.

Plack. Why yes!—I've rais'd and laid five hundred in my time.

Top. (*Aside.*) That's true enough, my girl! but I'll secure the spit for fear of the worst.

Rac. Oh! my dear pet, do lay him den.

Plack. Have you courage enough to see him, dear Cooney?

Rac. No, no, no, no!—dear pet.

Plack. But there no avoiding it now, you'll see him only in part.

Rac. Oh! oh! oh! (*Trembling.*) I bish he was gone!

Plack. (*Places Raccoon's back towards the bed.*) Stand you here; don't stir an inch, bend your head a little that way, you may shut your eyes—he's visible, but don't be afraid, he shan't hurt you. (*She beckons to Topinlift, he comes from under the bed, she meets him and puts an old blue petticoat over his head and shoulders, and reads.*) Dunder unt vetter schleemer hoont, ein blixum kindt, risum teneatis amissee (*Topinlift oversets Raccoon, drops the spit, and runs off.*)

Rac. (*Looking frighten'd.*) Mercey on me, here am I? Oh! oh!

Plack. Get up, dear Cooney!—did you see him?—you an't hurt I hope, my dear!—let me help you up. (*She raises him*) don't be frighten'd, he'll trouble you no more, he's a thousand leagues off by this time. (*She applies a smelling bottle to his nose, he starts.*)

Rac. Oh! my dear pet! I—I—I nebber was so frighten'd in all my life; is he gone?

Plack. Aye, far enough—didn't you see him go?

Rac. I hab de glimp of him as he goed by, I tought he did carry away de corner of de house wid him. Oh! o'!

Plack. (*Runs to the bottle, and brings him a dram.*) Drink this, dear Cooney, and you'll soon recover your spirits.

Rac. (*Trembling, drinks.*) Oh! I was'nt not afraid, a—a—only——

Plack. Courage man!—you'll see ten times more before morning!

Rac. I tink he look like de sailor.

Plack. Yes!—why he's the apparition of one of Blackbeard's crew, and as a confirmation that you'll obtain the treasure, he threw, that spit on the floor as he went off.

Rac (*Takes up the spit*) Why dis is de bery spit dat I put under de bed!

Plack So much the better, it was a signal to be gone.

Rac Well, I get de pick-ax and de spade, and den I'll go, but I must have dis liddle book to show Mr. Rattletrap.

Plack No, no—it's high Dutch, he can't read it. (*Takes it from him.*)

Rac. (*Goes to the bed and takes the pick-axe and spade.*) Now one buss, my dear pet, and den——

[*Kisses her and sings.*

SONG XIV.

Oh! when I get de welt,
Dat's buried by de mill,
Enjoy long life an helt,
An pleasure at my will.

What ſtore of gold I'll bring,
My lovely pet to dee,
Den none but my poor ting
Shall ſhare de ſame wid me. [*Exit Raccoon.*

Plac. Well,—it's an old ſaying, and I think a true one:—When poverty comes in at the door, love flies out at the window. Really I have experienced the truth of it lately, and hadn't it been for Topinlift, and a few tranſient friends, I ſhou'd have been in a poor ſituation; for I'm ſure Raccoon's nothing belonging to him that can pleaſe me but his money, and I ſee very little of that. He promiſes mountains of gold! but I fancy he'll be deceived as well as myſelf! I'll truſt no longer to bare promiſes, when a woman finds herſelf deceived, and deprived of moſt of the comforts of life, ſhe has it always in her power, and ſhe muſt be a fool, if ſhe don't take her revenge in a way the moſt pleaſing to herſelf. [*Sings.*

SONG XV.

Sure gold is the fuel that kindles the fire,
And ſerves for to fan up a woman's deſire,
To a fumbling fool that's decrepid and old:
For in all ſcenes of life, from the great to the little,
The bench, bar and pulpit, it ſuits to a tittle;
You're ſurely condemn'd, if you hav'n't the gold.
But if you have money, ne'er mind what your cauſe is,
But tickle their palms and you'll gain their applauſes;
No ſtateſman ſo great, ſo cunning, and bold,
But will truckle to you, for the ſake of your gold;
And ſhou'd you lack that—you are certainly ſold.
But hang this diſappointment!
Let women of bus'neſs take care of their men,
If one won't ſuffice them—why, let them have ten.
[*Exit.*

SCENE V. *A Room at Mrs. Trushoop's.*

Mrs. Truf Here he cums!—poor fowl!—how magre he looks! I vow to St. Patrick! an I pity him!

(*Enter* TRUSHOOP *and* DOLLY.)

(MRS TRUSHOOP *meeting him with a bowl of punch.*)

Truf And was you after wanting me, my deer?

Mrs. Truf. To be fure an I was, honey, an hares to you my jewel, and fuffex to your undertakins, dare! (*Drinks*)

Truf I thank you kindly, my deer!—but I don't know what you mane!

Mrs. Truf Never mind! drink hearty! (*Drinks.*) Take anudder pull at it, dare! (*Drinks again.*) Shure! an it's vary good punch.

Truf. By my fowl!—and it is fo, it drinks for all the world like nectar-ambrofial! fo it does.

Mrs. Truf Cum give me one of your fwate ould fafhion kiffes, dare! (*Kiffes him*) troth, an it feems like ould times now, juft for all the wurld—let me take off your apern, honey, for fhure an you'll have no more 'cafion for it after this. (*She takes off his apron and throws it from her.*)

Truf Why now, deer!—an what do you mane?

Mrs Truf. Never mind, fit down, honey! fure an you muft be vary hungry?

Truf. Indeed, and I am fo!

Mrs. Truf. Poor fowl!—Dolly cum hither child.

Dolly. Here! ma'am.

Mrs Truf. Here, my good child, take the kays an the big market bafket, an go your ways an open the pantry, an fetch up them two cowl roaft ducks.—

Dolly. Yes, ma'am!

Mrs. Truf An the capers—

Dolly. Yes, ma'am!

Mrs Truf. An the anchobies, an the gammon—

Dolly Yes, ma'am! (*Going.*)

Truf (*Aside, looking surpris'd*) By my sowl! this looks well on ou ... !

Mrs Truf. Come hither girl! is your going without half you arrant; an the packeid sammon, an the horse-raddish, an the cowl roast-beef—

Dolly Yes, ma'am. (*Going.*)

Truf. (*Aside.*) Augh hoogh! better and better.

Mrs Truf Stop girl! I say—don't be in such a hurry, an the kagg of lobsters the pickel'd seeters, an the swate-oyl, you know your masster loves oyl, an it's vary ha'ing to the belly ——

Dolly (*Smiling aside.*) Yes, ma'am—any thing else?

Mrs. Truf. Why yes, hussey! the jarr of olives—the Chaster chize—the nates-tung, the sous'd rock, the potted pigeons, the apple-pie, the cowl potatoes, the whiskey-jugg, an a hunder'd things more, but do that first.

Dolly. (*Smiling aside.*) Why ma'am! this big basket won't hold the half of them!

Mrs. Truf. Why then, go an fetch the tother big basket, you fool you! have you no contraption?

Dolly. (*Going and laughing aside.*) Hah! hah! hah! Well, I wonder what all this means? for this week past she's been starving him, and now she's going to cram him like a stuff'd turkey! I believe in my conscience, she's light-headed! [*Exit Dolly.*

Truf. Blassings on you, dee! but you're too good. Why now, when you are good, why then you are too good!

Mrs. Truf. No indeed! an indeed! an I an't, I can't be good enuff—faith! an you desarve it all an more too.—Shall I send for some sassages an aggs? an will you have a nice ſpare-rib broyl'd, with ſome apple ſauce, honey?

Truſ. No fath, deer! I think in my conſhence and heres enuff! why now, if I was an allephant, I cou dn't ate the half of it? ſo I cou'd!

Mrs. Truſt. Shure, but you muſt be vary hungry!

Truſ. Fath! an I am ſo an I more too, but I muſh't make a beaſt of myſelf for all that! you know, deer!

(*Enter* DOLLY, *with the two big market baſkets heaped up.*)

Mrs Truſ. An have you forgot ev'ry thing, girl?

Dolly. Yes, ma'am.

Mrs Truſ. Why then fatch them in the parler, an lay the damaſk table cloth on the big table girl, an ſet it off han'ſome an nate, your maaſter ſhall ſup in the parler, ſo he ſhall; an when your done all that, why, go your ways preſently, (not juſt now) an warm my bed vary well, an ſprad the curtins, do you hare, I ſay?

Dolly Yes, ma'am. [*Exit Dolly.*

Truſ Indeed, my deer! and I'm vary ſorry, you give yourſelf a grate dale of trubble for me!

Mrs. Truſ. No, indeed honey, an I do not!—an you know I was always plaz'd to ſee you ate harty.

Truſ Yes, my deer—but I forgot it lately!

Mrs. Truſ. Well! never mind it dare, I wiſh you good luck in your undertakins.

Truſ. I thank you my deer,—but what wou'd you be after now?

Mrs. Truſ Augh, fath!—the trazure, to be ſhure!

Truſ What trazure?

Mrs. Truſ. Cum—cum, don't think to kape it a ſacret from me—ſhure an I know all about it now!

Truſ. About what pray?

Mrs. Truſ Hav'n't I towld you now?

Truſ. (*aſide*) By my ſowl! and we're all ruin'd, ſome traytor has blow'd us! Some nonſenſe in your head.

Mrs. Truf. Faith! an it isn't nonsense though—shure an Mrs. Trowell towld me all about it—as how you are going to dig for trazure, an a graite dale more—

Truf. And how does Mrs. Trowell know?

Mrs. Truf. Faith! an vary well, shure an Trowell towld her all about it.

Truf. Augh! the book-sworn? oath-breaking dog! oh! the traitor! oh! the Judas! Augh! and Trowell and you must do grait pannance for all this. Well, thank God! and I'm not book-sworn!

Mrs. Truf. No, my dare, no more you arn't; cum, never mind honey, let's go into supper.

Truf. I'll follow, deer. (*Aside.*) Augh! the slubber-degullion dog! [*Exeunt.*

SCENE VI. *A Room.*

(*Enter* DOLLY, *with a warming pan, and* TERRANCE *meeting her.*)

Dolly. Oh! Terrance—I'm glad you're come! he! he! he!

Ter. I suppose so! you want me to fatch a bucket of vater, an then kiss you? don't you? say? (*Chucking her under the chin—Kisses her.*)

Dolly. No faith! I don't—but here's the devil to pay! he! he! you never saw the like in all your born days!

Ter. What?—what the devil is it?——

Dolly. Why you must go and fetch the priest! he! he! master and mistress has made it up, and they're going to be married over again!

Ter. Hoot! the girl tawks like a fool!!

Dolly. No faith! I don't, the wedding supper's on the table, and she's going to make him eat our two great big market baskets full, all up at once, and faith! I don't know but the baskets in the bargain he! he!

Ter. By my fowl! Dolly but I believe your'e crazy! —or

Dolly. No, I an't!—you fool!—but you can't think, how kind she has been to him, kissing and slobbering his chops about, like all the world—and the Lord! knows what, and treating him with punch—but I watch'd her, and she took care to have the largest share to herself.

Ter. Fath!—but I believe an you had a large share too, by your tawk.

Dolly. No—the devil a drop I got of it!

Ter. Then your'e humbugging me, arn't you now Dolly?

Dolly. No, I an't 'pon honor!—only peep thro' the key-hole, and see what an elegant variety there is, for the wedding supper!

Ter. Hoot you fool!

Dolly. Peep thro' here!—can't you?

Ter. *(Peeps.)* Oh! Jasus!—a grate faste by my fowl! —shure enuff!—why there's enuff for the howl Kongrass!—an nobody to ate it! the divil burn me!—but I'll have sum of it!—if they don't ate it all! but what the divil's all this for? say Dolly?

Dolly. The Lord above knows!—I swear! I don't, no more than a horse!—if I did, I would tell you indeed, Terrance—We shall know more about it to-morrow, I think.

Ter. The forerunner of anudder dam'd quarrel!

Dolly. The devil may care for me!

Ter. An me too—but sure Dolly, an you can tell us a little more, about the maning of it?

Dolly. No faith! I can't—only mistress went over the way this evening, to drink tea with Mrs. Trowell, and presently after, she came running home, quite out of breath, and bawl'd out, like a mad cow, bawling for her calf!—Dolly!—Dolly! three or four times,

(I thought the houſe had been on fire!—or ſome develiſh thing, or, other) and ordered me to put on the tea-kettle, in all haſte—and Oh! how ſhe bothered me, ſhe wanted it to boil, before the fire was made,—Lord! how vex'd I was—I could have cut her throat!—"does it boil?—does it boil?—make haſte girl!—how long you ſtay?—what are you poking about?"—*(mimicking her)* and called me baggage, and trollop, and a hundred bad names, you never heard ſuch a Billingſgate!—I never was ſo curſedly vext, and blinded with ſmoke, in all my life,—and was obliged at laſt to bring in the tea-kettle as it was, and the devil a boil it boil'd no more than when I firſt put it on the fire—ſo I don't care!

Ter. An ſerve her rate too—the owl'd Jazzebel!

Doll. But the beauty of it was, Terrance,—ſhe made me take the two big market baſkets, and go down into the cellar, and fetch up every thing there, for maſter to eat and drink, (faith! I almoſt broke my back with them, they were ſo heavy)—and call him out of the ſhop?—Oh! you never ſee ſuch a fidgetting as ſhe made!—

Ter. I'll warrant the Brimſtone made noyſe enuff! faith! an ſhe's no ſlouch at that! let's have anudder peep at um—Augh hoogh! an how he tares away at the roaſt ducks?

Doll. I don't at all wonder at it—he's almoſt ſtarv'd!

Ter. By my ſowl!—but this is a queer ſort of a ſeveriuſhin—here's ſomething brewing, Dolly! take my word for it, but what are you after wid the wharming-pan?

Doll. Why you fool!—what do you think, when people's married? why they're going to bed together after ſupper, and ſhe ordered me to warm it.

Ter. Worse an worse—by my sowl!—but there'll be a grate earthquake to-night! I expact—but you slut you, why you hav'n't been up yet to warm it, an the pans quite cowl'd

Dolly. Faith! I don't care! then let 'em lye the cloler and warm it themselves

Ter. Hah! hah! hah!—[illegible]

Dolly. Oh! gracious—they're coming to bed!—Run Terrance! don't let 'em see you for all the world!—hide yourself in the cow-house, and when they're gone to bed, we'll partake of the wedding feast

Ter. That's rite Dolly—I'm divilish hungry and dry too!

Dolly. I wont forget you, fly you devil!—fly! they are here. [*Exit Terrance.*

(*Enter* MR. *and* MRS. TRU[illegible], *with a candle, meeting* DOLLY.)

Mrs Trus. An have you now, warm'd the bed well girl?

Dolly. Yes ma'am, very well.

Mrs Trus. And sprad the Kurtins?

Dolly. Yes ma'am.

Mrs Trus. Then go your ways, an clare the table, an put out the fire, and lock the dure, an go your ways bed.

Dolly. Yes ma'am.

Mrs Trus. Where's Terrance?

Dolly. Gone to bed ma'am.

Mrs Trus. How long first?

Dolly. Two hours ago ma'am.

Mrs Trus. How cum that?

Dolly. He said he was sleepy ma'am

Mrs Trus. Vary well, go your ways

Dolly. Yes ma'am, (*Aside*) blatherum, *lolling out her tongue and* [*Exeunt.*

ACT III. SCENE I. *The place of action, near the Mill and Stone-bridge.*

(Scene opens and discovers RATTLETRAP *dress'd in his magic habit, with a dark lanthorn and candle,* QUADRANT, *with a magnet, rod, and wand, &c. &c. &c. an old iron bound [illegible], and* SPITFIRE, *with a copper figure, representing the head and shoulders of* BLACKBEARD.*)*

Rat. Well done Spitfire! the hole I see is made.

Sp. Yes—yes—I've not been idle, since you left me.

Quad. (Aside) He's the very plan of a fellow!

Rat. (Aside) Not his fellow to be found—He has performed wonders!—But we must lose no time, *(looks at his watch)* 'tis near eleven o'clock. *(They poke in the right [illegible], br[illegible] [illegible] letters, and two or three rusty [illegible] of [illegible])*

Quad. Come! come! let's bury it at once. *(All assist, and bury the chest.)*

Rat. (To Spitfire) Now we've nothing more to do, at present, than to see you descend into your subterraneity —step down!—step down! and mind when I give the signal, throw fire-balls, and when they come to a sight of the chest, push up the figure, and act as I have before directed you——Now be sure you act the devil, as if you were going to deceive the devil himself, and we'll reward you devilishly well.

Spit. And the devil take me if I don't! *(Spitfire goes down the hole, and takes the figure, lanthern, and candle with him.)*

Quad. Now every thing is ready to receive them, and if our devil plays his part well—I think, we shall have a devilish merry night of it. He! he! he!—egad here's some of 'em coming! *(They halloo without, Canoe! Canoe! those within answer, Canoe! Canoe!)*

(Enter HUM *and* PARCHMENT.*)*

Rat. Where are the mud-mongers?

Parch. They're just at hand, we heard them, as we came down the hill. *(Different voices within hallooing Canoe! Canoe! Canoe! Canoe! &c. [illegible] within answering Canoe! &c.)*

(Enter WASHBALL, TRUSHOOP, BUCKRAM, RACCOON *and* TROWELL, *with pick-axes, spades, shovels, spits, and* ANDRA FERRARA *[illegible].)*

Wash. I tore my shirt unaccountably, coming thro' the briers!

Trus. Faith! and I tumbled up the hill, 'till I got my futt in the boggs, and if I hadn't held fast by the vater, I'd be drown'd.

Hum and Quad. Hah! Hah! he! he!

Rac. Don't mind, gentlemen, what is de tore [illegible], or de co'ld foot, compar'd wid de prospect of dese riches?

Buck. By me saul! mon—and I chearg'd mesel we twa bottles to leeghten me nawse, and thats a bonny guede in a dark neeght, and for fear o meeting wi ony skoondrels, Ize fee ch'd me Andra wi me, a gude stiff as e'er [illegible] made in a scotland!

Rat. Well gentlemen, I see we're all here, don't let us waste time, let's b[illegible] keep silence! by the calculation I made this morning, by the [illegible]ellites, the treasure must be near [illegible] place, *([illegible])* [illegible] magnet works this way——

Rac. I tought so.

Trus. La[illegible] your [illegible]ation!

Rat. [illegible] it draws excessive strong [illegible] way [illegible] I feel myself interrupted b[illegible] I can [illegible] keep [illegible] rod in my hand, there! now I have [illegible]

R[illegible] [illegible] place, gentlemen!

Trus. And can't you now be aisey, and howl'd your tung? you fool! you know nothing about it.

Wash. Oh! dear! what interruptions?

Rat. Not a word! not a word! pray be silent! I'm near the place, the rod points to this spot—I'm near the centre, I know the rod to be true, I've tried its virtue, 'twas cut on All-hallows eve, at 12 o'clock at night, with my back to the moon, and the mercury injected while the sap was running.

Trus. (*Aside.*) By the holy stone! but I believe, he was born in the moon!

Rat. (*Draws a large circle with his wand, and says*) Diapaculum interravo, tenebrossitas stravaganza! (*Goes round the circle, and sticks twelve pieces of iron-wire in the Periphery, each piece having a bit of paper cut out in the form of a star on its head—as he sticks them down, he names the twelve signs of the Zodiac.*) Aries, Taurus, Germini, Cancer, Leo, Virgo, Libra, Scorpio, Sagitarius, Capriconius, Aquarius, Pisces, make no noise else you'll disturb Jupiter, who is the most wakeful planet, and is now in his first sleep. (*He puts on a large pair of spectacles.*) Let me see! its now 12 o'clock, Jupiter in a sound sleep, a good omen! (*He calls* WASHBALL, TRUSHOOT, BUCKRAM, RACOOON, *and* TROWELL.) Take off your coats and jackets, (*they pull them off*) now stand within the circle, (*he places* HUB, QUADRANT, *and* PARCHMENT, *without the circle, at different posts, and says*) now keep a good look out, Canoe's the word, so don't forget it.

Trus. (*Aside.*) The devil a forget, myself will forget! faith! and I will sooner forget my prayers!

Rat. Now run down the spit and try this place—Mr. Washball.

Wash. (*Thrusts down the spit, and says.*) Oh dear! it's very soft and slushey.

Rat. Never mind! the better digging,—try it again, I know its the identical spot!

Wash. Softer and softer, I feel it! I feel it! it strikes against something!

Rat. Then fall too all hands, and dig, and when the watch-word is given, fall flat on the ground (*They dig, he views the stars*) now the Dragons head and the Scorpion's tail are in conjunction Castor's in the wane, Procyon is stationary, but Sagitarius seems obnubilated, and fast approaching to a state of obtenebration! hah! I don't like that! it rather looks inauspicious and portentous of ill!—but Syrius's right foot——

Pick (*W[illegible]*) C[illegible]oe! (*Th[illegible] ans[illegible] [illegible] and fall down with n the c[illegible] A [illegible] heard at a distan[illegible], playing [illegible]*)

Rat Inferno atum, gastro fagrum!—R[illegible]se and go on! 'twas nothing but a blind drunken fidler, and some company returning from Batchelors-hall!

Trus By my sow[illegible] now, and I've made a [illegible] jackle of my se[illegible]f, all over full of mud! Augh! and I had the spawlpene here [illegible]n I'd give him two or three handfulls of bothers w[illegible]d my [illegible], so I wou'd'nt.

Bac[illegible] Deel [illegible]ak me mon! bu[illegible] I diana leke this, 'tis a foul drum[illegible]ic p'ecce, gin I a wa[illegible] h[illegible]m, I [illegible] claw the [illegible]y ke a wee bit, and brok his d[illegible] d feedle!

W[illegible] Ah me!

R[illegible] Not a word gentlemen! proceed, (*th[illegible] [illegible]*) but Syrius's right foot, over O[illegible]ion's left shoulder, looks well, and the Swan's tail near the H[illegible]'s heart, has a promising appearance (*Or[illegible] [illegible], the diggers frighten'd and attemp[illegible] to run out of the c[illegible]*) Don't stir an inch! if you break the mounds, I've no power!—dig! dig! Conj[illegible]bctin[illegible], morentiu[illegible]n [illegible]habavo, omnibusque contubern[illegible]n! [illegible] th[illegible]s leap-year [illegible] not unfavorable. (*[illegible] fire-ba[illegible], with a roaring [illegible], at wh[illegible] they are terrified.*)

Tr[illegible] (*[illegible]*) A[illegible]gh! how my ha[illegible]t bates!

Waſh. Come near Mr Rattletrap! Oh! dear! Oh! dear! I ſhall faint!

Trow. I'd give all my ſhare, I had never come! mercy on me!

Rac. Oh! Oh!—I wiſh I was at home, I nebber wou'd come again!

Buck. Hoot! canna ye a be queeit?

Rat. Never fear! I'll protect you!—Hobonos cum verigos, omne croxibus nduvientum! dig! dig! (*viewing the ſtars*) but yet certain appearances, puts me to a ſtand, baffles my utmoſt ſkill, and indicates an infernal oppoſition! I'll try my Omphaloptic glaſs. Aye! now I diſcover the cauſe of the oppoſition! I now diſtinctly perceive, thro' a boundleſs radiant apperture, the tail of a huge Comet! like a monſtrous, overgrown ram-cat, with his hind legs, kicking and ſcratching the Planets and Stars about, as tho' they were marbles or ſnow-balls! ſtrange Phenomenon! a glorious opportunity this would be, for a young divine, to ſtudy Aſtro-Theology! one peep thro' this, would inſtantaneouſly and eternally ſilence, the whole hoſt of ſceptics!

" Fierce meteors ſhoot their arbitrary light
And Comets march with lawleſs horrors bright!"

[illegible] (*Without*) Canoe! (*All anſwer Canoe! and fall down.*)

Rat. Metamulorabulum, exultiſſimo ccalu'um mongraco! Riſe! it was nothing but an old cow paſſing along! go on! (*All ſ[illegible] ſtaring.*)

Buck. Damn the Hawkie for a dorty beech! wha the deel does ſhe want here? does ſhe tak us for Bulls an be damn'd to her?

Trow. Arra dear! and how my wife will ſcowld, when I fatch her one money, for ſpiling my new brogues.

Rat. Sagittarius is now clear, and the Orb of the

Moon, is in contact with Jupiter, good! Sextile in conjunction with Quartile right! (*He waves his wand.*) Saturn is a metallic planet, and tho' in common the most dull, is now perfectly pellucid, and out shines even Venus herself! this is the best sign of all! (*Another fire-ball, a roaring below.*)

Wash. Oh! dear! Oh dear!

Rac. Oh! Oh! Oh!—what shall I do?

Iri. Defend us! defend us!—Mr. Rattletrap!—Oh!—

Rat. These invisibles would disturb you awhile, now your just upon it. Conjunction, oppositorium, placabulum somoso!—dig away! Arcturus now appears, Constellatione planetarum! Venus is now the morning star, and is eclipsed four digits (*[illegible] fire-balls, and a roaring below, they [illegible] terrified.*) Now their rage increases! we'er near the treasure, don't be afraid, I am with you, their fiery darts will soon be over, dig! dig! Cummeritantibus considerationibus, terrabandum ophagnum!

Wash. Oh!—Oh!—Oh!—

Back. Quit mon! quit! wha the deel cares for em, dig mon! dig!

Rac. Oh!—Oh!—what will become of us?

Rat. Stick to it!—Stick to it! (*They dig.*) These nocturnal observations, sometimes deceive the brightest astronomers! the whole planetary system now changes and appears to have a centrifugal motion—now whirls within a huge vortex, with a velocity, beyond the power of mathematics to calculate, now orbicular! now circumvolves! and Georgium Sidus, forms an obtuse angle, whose Hypothenuse seems offuscated, or eclipsed by the horns of the Moon, and whose perpendicular is geocentric with our earth! these appearances are new to me—beyond my Talismanic powers to comprehend! preternatural! utterly unnexcogitable! In shot, I have never experienced such a rare Synchronism, since I have had any knowledge of the Occult sciences! however I now perceive a ray of hope! Hecetius Doccius! now Cassiopæa and the Bears-tail, are on the meridian! excessive lucky!

Hum. (*Aside*) He performs to admiration!

Quad (*Aside*) Incomparably well, by Jupiter! He! he! he! (*Two or three fire balls, and an increase of roaring below.*)

Wash. Mercy on me! I shall faint—Oh! oh!

Ed. Haud up mon!

Rac. O my poor ting, I wish I had stay'd wid you!

Trow. I tremble every joint of me. O Lord! oh!

Tush (*Aside*) Faith! and my knees thump togedder, like a pair of pot-hooks, but I won't tell um for all that.

Rat. Gentlemen!—summon up all your courage!—don't be pusillanimous! dig! dig!—the enemy's fire is nearly exhausted!—Tincturum, corrosivum, sublimatum! (*Takes an [illegible]*)

Quad (*Without, aside*) Come let's drink while the fools are digging. He! he! he! (*They drink, and point, and laugh at the diggers.*) Poisonous exhalations rise from this devilish swamp! I'm afraid old Washball will get the Cholera-morbus. He! he! he!

Parch (*Without, aside*) I'm rather of opinion he'll get the Perip-no-money. Ha! ha!

Hum (*Without, aside*) By the Lord Harry! that's well said! I'm entirely of your opinion—no money. Ha! ha! ha!

Rat. Every thing now looks well! fine appearances! Spica, south eleven degrees fifty eight minutes, good! to-morrow is Sexagesima sunday, good! Lyra, south, sets nine minutes after one this morning, good! the horns of the moon in Apogee, good! Bull's-eye rises, good again! Venus rises, very good! she sets S. West obliquely towards the mines of Mexico and Peru, excellent! In short! the macrocosm of the whole visible system of nature, are strongly in our favor! a certain sign of success! occidental! occidental! glorious!

Truf. (*Aside*) By St. Patrick! but I swatt swately!—by my sowl! now but its harder work than digging paratoe!

Tre. (*Aside*) Only see how it drops off me! I wish it was all over

Truf. (*Aside*) It's good for your helt, you devil you Fath! and I would be very sorry, but I had one good drink of whiskey just now my deer.

Rat. Have a little patience! the bull's eye is this moment stationary and opacous! it would prove fatal to drink now! it would most assuredly bring on the Hydrophobia! dig! dig! before the eclipse comes on! our success altogether depends upon your industry, one second of time now well employ'd, is worth a whole year! go on! go on! redouble your vigilance!

Patch (*Aside, without*) Let's give 'em another tumble in the mud

Quad. (*Without, aside*) With all my heart,—he! he!—Canoe! (*The diggers answer Canoe! and fall down*)

Rat. Facinorum, muddum, dashum, splashum. Rise and go on! it was nothing but a distant barking of dogs (*Viewing the stars.*)

Wash Oh dear! I can't support it any longer! it will kill me! indeed it will! these cursed dog days are coming fast upon us!

Truf. By my sowl and you're right—fath an they bark all night long in our alley!—O Jasus! and what a packle I'm in?

Hum, Patch, and Quad (*Without, aside*) Hah! hah! he! he! (*alternately*)

Rat Benedictum, atmosphericum! hold out only six minutes, three quarters and the 197th part of a minute and we have it! (*Pointing to the stars with his wand*) luckily for us! the star Wormwood (as mentioned in the Revelations) is in a state of occultation! Mars approaching omnoleney! and Bacchus as drunk as a piper, success is certain! (*Fire-balls and a terrible roaring.*)

Wash Oh! I'm dead! I'm dead!

Rat I'll soon vivificate you! here, take a little Aqua me Rabulus, it cost me half a crown a spoonful. (*He drinks it off*)

Truf Stop! stop! don't drink it all!

Trow. You needn't halloo to him, don't you know a man can't hear while he's drinking?

Truf Faith an I never know'd that before! by my sowl next time I'll be up wid him, and I'll halloo, stop, stop you devil you, afore he begins.

Buck That's reeght mon!

Wash. How it revives the animal spirits?

Truf. The devil burst you, and that's all the harm I wish you!

Rat (*Aside*) Ha! ha!—(*Looks at his watch*) the time's just expired—pray be serious! dig away! dig away! now for your lives! I feel the ground move under my feet!—the treasure is struggling, it wants to be relieved from it's long imprisonment, dig!—dig!—Theophrasticum, Privilegium! now the whole host of devils are pulling against us, and levelling all the darts of infernal fury at us!

Trow. I feel the chest!—I feel the chest!

Wash. I see it! I see it!

Rat. Ne plus ultra! up with it, up with it, all's our own! (*The ghost appears and spits fire, the diggers with uplifted hands, looking at it.*)

Trow How he squints.

Buck. The deel me care! troth mon an he looks leke auld Squintesego at Aberdeen!

Truf. Faith an he squints sure enuff, but no more

than a [illegible] to [illegible] m[illegible] how [illegible] out [illegible] as [illegible] no [illegible] how!

[illegible] I [illegible]

R. [illegible] H[illegible] his [illegible] ofe like a band-[illegible] he [illegible]

T. [illegible] by [illegible], and [illegible] me!

H. He [illegible] a Co[illegible] after [illegible] ap-pearance, [illegible] manage him for [illegible]! (*[illegible]*)

H. O! what an old fool [illegible] I have been—I've brought myfelf into a fad fcrape! Mea culpa——

R. Pray in Englifh! pray in Englifh! de [illegible] fpirits don't underftand de latin [illegible] O! O! I don't know what to [illegible] O! O! I [illegible] I hab I b'd a better life do Mr [illegible] power!

W. De [illegible], domine! I can't pray in [illegible], do you fay fomething [illegible] O! Mr [illegible] I'm dead! I'm dead. Oh! O! [illegible]

H. Lord! [illegible] mercy [illegible] and keep [illegible] from us! O! how my [illegible] to break de Perr[illegible]!

P. Crucifixarum, Ad[illegible] Per[illegible]orum! [illegible] H[illegible] almoft conquer'd now!

R. Right worfhipful mafter, no—As it was in de beginning—no, no, what is your name? Raccoon, who gib you dat name? my grand-moder and god-fader, no dats wrong—Our fader—I can't fay it! Oh! Oh!

G

Oh! for eber and eber, Amen. Dare he comes, dare he comes again!

Truf (To Raccoon) Lave off you black-mout! you havn't it, (*he says*) Pater-nofter, mea culpa, Sinnerorum, helpum, deliverum, miſſerabulum, tuſcarorum

Buck By me faul mon! 'tis the deel himfel! I ee fee his claven foot!—(*Aside*) Troth and he makes me quack too, a wee-pickle!

Trow. Save us! Save us! from his fiery jaws! he's feeking whom he may devour.

Truf Augh! and if he fwallows me, by my fowl! and I'll kick his guts out in the twinkling of a broom-ſtick!

Waſh Oh! Oh! fave me!—fave me too!

Rat. (To the ghoſt) Superiorum, lakeavi, hurorum! *(The ghoſt diſappears)* now's the lucky minute, the Serpent's-neck, is round the Poleaſter! Raiſe the cheſt, (*They riſe, the ghoſt appears, and ſpits fire, with fire-balls, the roaring below increaſes, the diggers ſhrieking and trembling, thoſe without laugh at them*) Now, gentlemen, raiſe the cheſt, baniſh fear! keep faſt! (*he calls to thoſe without*) your aſſiſtance gentlemen or we loſe all! ſhou'd it ſink now, it's irrecoverably loſt! not all the magicians of Egypt, nor the witch of Endor cou'dn't recover it! quick gentlemen! quick! nows the intereſting moment!

"There is a tide in the affairs of men,
"Which if taken at the flood, leads on to fortune."

up with it. *(They run and aſſiſt in raiſing the cheſt.)*

Rac. (*Looking towards the ghoſt*) Dats Old Blackbeard himſelf! by de birtue and de power of de free and de accepted maſon, to me gibben, (*here he gives the free-maſon's ſign, or ſomething like it*) I command you to depart! Oh! Oh! Oh what diſturbs dy poor ſoul from reſt?

Rat. Horrificatabus, Profundum, Horridumque, Spectaculum, Demonium.

Buck. Haud taut, dinna quat yere grup, (*he steps towards the ghost*) noo I've ken him, I've gang after him.

[illegible] Pray don't Mr Buckram, it be de pirate apparition, and don't you see how bery angry he look at me, when I did speak to him?

T[illegible]. The devil be from me, and I believe its Doctor Foster!

Buck. The deel ma care, wha he be, Doctor Faustus, spirit, apparition, Blackbeard, or the deel himsel, gin he can stand a cut o me Andra, he mun be the deel in truth (*He takes up a broad sword, runs towards the ghost, makes a cut at it, and falls down, the ghost disappears for a short time, returns again spitting fire, the roaring continues more violent. Buckram lies on the ground, at last says*) Deil tak a warlocks I say, I ha leek to ha brok my necke down the brae!

Teag. By my sowl! and you'd like to make a Somersault of it! faith! and Ricketts is a nincompoop to you honey!

Rat. (*aside*) Ha! ha! ha! a comical dog.—That was a very impetuous, temerarious step! didn't you know he's invulnerable? if I hadn't been here, you would have been incinerated, for your presumption. (*He steps up to the ghost, and says*) Horridum, Callesindum, Buscantivo, Interdenabulum! thus far will I permit thee to come, but no farther. Avaunt! Avaunt! Avaunt! and be thou laid in Lake Huron! 'till the waters thereof be exhausted! (*The ghost disappears, with a dreadful noise*) now we're all safe! Consummatum et Triumphicatibus! up with the chest! those fiends of darkness will trouble us no more.

Buck. (*Rises up and shakes himself*) The deel a feoght mare, ye'ell ha o him noo he's gatten a smell o me

Andra! (*they burſt up the cheſt, ſome black ruſty pieces of ſilver tumble out.*)

Rat. Now our toils are over, and we have caught our prey.

All. Huzza! huzza! huzza! &c.

Waſh. (*Greedily taking up one of the pieces of ſilver, kiſſes it and ſays*) Oh! my dear! my dear! (*he puts it and takes it to the lanthorn.*) Let me ſee—(*puts on his ſpectacles*) One Thouſand, Sixteen Hundred and Eighty Four, aye! aye! this is the very money, that Blackbeard got at Panama, when he robb'd the churches! Oh! the poor prieſts! the poor prieſts! It ſeems very providentially to have fallen into my hands! Come! come! let's take it away, before day-light appears.

Hum. May we preſume to take it away, Mr. Rattletrap?

Rat. Jubileetatebuſque!—Finis cum fiſtulum, populorum jigg!—my buſineſs is finiſhed, therefore all's our own! away with it!

Hum. There's one thing proper firſt to mention, gentlemen, my ſiſter from whom I received the information, and to whom we are all ſo much indebted for this lucky turn of good fortune, is entitled to a ſhare; beſides, I think ſhe highly merits a handſome gratuitous preſent, as an acknowledgment of our gratitude to her.

Rac. No, brudder Hum, I tink ſhe's titled to no more den half de ſhare, ſhe's no more den de woman. But, what do you mean by de preſent?

Hum. A whole ſhare! I inſiſt upon it, is her juſt due! but, as for the preſent, that muſt be left to your generoſity, and I dare anſwer you'll not be wanting in munificence! what think you of one of the boxes of diamonds, or ſome ſuch trifle?

Rat. By all means!

Patch. Little enough in all conscience!

Quad. I think so indeed! I would add one of the boxes of pearls to it!

Wash. Lord! Lord! no, no; I protest against a share and a present too! we shall be ruin'd! ruin'd! Mr. Raccoon, indeed we shall, speak to 'em, do sir, do!

B—k. Damme mon! but I thin the lasie deserves em a, an mare too!

Rat. Consider! gentlemen, we hab run de risk of our libes wid dese spirits! besides, what will de woman do wid so much of de dimonts, and de oder tings?

Wash. Aye, indeed! I say the diamonds truly! why they are of more value than all the rest of the things together! why you are all going mad!—mad!—mad!—indeed you are!

Irish. Faith an' she shall have um all for me! and more too! by my sowl! but I believe and you want 'um all yourself to hang up at your shop-winder, to make paple think how you're a toot-drawer, and don't you now, honey?

Parcn. Gentlemen, I'm surprized! nay, almost petrified, at this sudden change of sentiments you have now expressed! you, who before you were possessed of this immense treasure, entertained such lofty and laudable ideas of ambition, philanthropy and generosity! you, who were for purchasing titles, building and endowing hospitals and the Lord knows what! I say, gentlemen, I am astonish'd beyond measure at the change. Can it be possible! that you, who are now in actual possession of this treasure, you so ardently wished for; and I say, gentlemen, on the attainment of which your pious resolutions were founded, should so suddenly change and turn traitors to that heaven-born virtue, gratitude! and that Satan, that malignant, malicious, malevolent, mischievous, unpropitious, pestilential, pestiferous, envious, spiteful, ungrateful devil! could so suddenly transform you into such Judases, as even that most avaricious of all devils! Mammon himself! would blush at, hang down his head, and be ashamed of. I must not! I cannot believe it!

Wash. Mighty fine talk indeed! but its nothing but wind!

Trow. Come, come! let's give the poor woman a full share, and the diamonds and all; if it hadn't been for her we shou'dn't have had a copper!

Wash. No, no! I forbid it!—I protest against it!

Trus. (*Aside*) Hoot you owld brute.

Trow. Let's put it to a vote?

Hum. That's right! and should that fail I protest! I'll give my whole share to my sister, and phillippic them to petrifaction!

Rac. (*Aside, To Washball*) Who de debil's dis Philip Pick?

Wash. (*Aside*) I suppose some ruffian of a fellow! he's going to set upon us to way-lay, rob and murder us!

Rac. (*Aside.*) Yes, I tink so too! Dad I'll always carry my pistols in my pocket.

Quad. Vote! vote! (*They vote and carry it for a full share, and a present of a box of diamonds and a box of pearls.*)

Trus. Fath an I'm glad of it!

Hum. Gentlemen, I'm satisfy'd! and I heartily thank you in my sister's name.

Rac. I tink its a bery great shame!

Wash. Oh, dear!—we're ruin'd!—we're ruin'd!

Rat. The day approaches; remove it immediately!

Patch. Where shall we carry it?

Wash. There's a cunning place in my house, I'll take care of it! it will be safe! I'll sleep on it all night!

All say. Agreed!—agreed!

Hum. Now gentlemen, let's all meet precisely at six o'clock this morning and divide it. I think some of us shou'd assist Mr. Washball, as this chest contains an immense treasure, we can't be too careful, he's aged, and some unlucky circumstance may intervene.

Wash. No, no, I can take care of it, well enough.

Rat. Dat's right, brudder Hum, I tink I'd better go too, as I understand de military. If we should be attack, my service may be necessary.

Quad. Very true! and if Mr Trowell, Mr. Trushoop, and Mr. Buckram will attend you, it will be the safer.

Trus. The devil burn Trushoop, if he forsakes it!

Buck. Deel tak the mon, that lags beheend!

Rat. Well gentlemen! I think this great success, deserves a song; come bear chorus!

All say. With all my heart. [*Rattletrap sings.*

SONG XVI.

Tho' my art some despise, I appeal to your eyes,
For a proof of my magical knowledge,
Tho' the wisdom of schools, damn our art and our
tools,
We can laugh at the fools of the college.

Chorus. We can, &c.

Now my friends we're possest, of the glorious chest,
Join hands and rejoice beyond measure,

Let it be our first care, that great blessing to share,
Whose contents, are an infinite treasure!

Chorus. Whose, &c.

Now gentlemen bear off your prize!

Buck. Tak hau'd Trowel, I've hurt me shouther in the fa' i' gat down the brae—I canna carry't lad! (*The dupes take up the chest, and bear it off guarded by the humorists.*)

Wash. It feels brave and ponderous.

Trus. That's true for you!—faith! I woud'nt care if I break my back wid it. Arra dear! tread of my heels.

Trow. I beg your pardon!

Trus. Faith! an your very welcome—for the devil burn me, if I care for my heels at all, at all,—so I don't!—(*Exeunt omnes, Buckram brings up the rear, flourishing his broad sword, capering and singing a Scotch air.*)

SCENE, II. *A room in Washball's house.*

(*Enter* MEANWELL *and* LUCY.)

Lucy. Bless me! How could you venture (after the severe reproof my uncle gave you,) to approach this house, at this late hour of the night?

Mean. Love! angelic love! which knows no fear but your displeasure, hath brought me here on eagle's wings, to waft you hence, and seal that vow, already ratified in heaven!

Lucy. But consider my dear Meanwell, what may be the consequence of such a rash step, when, perhaps a few days perseverance, may bring it to a conclusion, with his consent.

Mean. I cannot think of trusting to any thing so precarious, and as he has already consented, by being my bondsman for the licence, and publicly declared his assent, we shall be looked upon by the honest, virtuous, and judicious, as sufficiently justified in taking this step.

Lucy I am confounded! my love to you spurs me to a flight! but my duty to my uncle, commands me to wait his reconciliation. I know not what to do, or, what to say!

Mean Haste! haste my dear Lucy! the precious moments are swiftly passing! each moment seems an hour 'till we're one, the clergyman waits, (with chosen friends) to tie the nuptial knot, and crown our bliss!

SONG XVII.

Lucy. My throbbing heart must now give way
To love, to honor, and obey
Lo! Hymen's torch is lighted
Lo! Hymen's, &c.

My heart! my all!—I now resign,
O! Meanwell!—Meanwell!—I'll be thine,
In wedlock's bands united!
In wedlocks, &c.

Mean. Of Venus' charms, let poets write!
Diana chaste, or, Juno bright!
Of Kitty, Doll, or, Susey!
Of Kitty, &c.

The charms of all, are center'd here,
In Lucy!—charming Lucy dear!
Haste! haste! my lovely Lucy!
Haste, &c.

[*They go off quick, hand in hand.*

SCENE III. *A Street.*

(*Enter* WASHBALL.)

Wash. I can't bear the thoughts of dividing, not I! division! why I cou'd never learn it at school! but, addition and multiplication, were always my darlings! Two hundred and fifty thousand pounds, divided into nine parts, let me see—aye! I have it! nine times nine is, a, a, sixty-two, no, that's wrong. Nine times eleven is, a, a hundred and six, and four over, no that's too much, but I'm no scholar, never mind, no matter,

I can count a hundred as fast as any of 'em, and they can't cheat me! Charity begins at home, and he must be the greatest fool on earth, that cheats himself, I never could forgive myself for such a sin as that, I think I am old enough to have more wit. He that cheats another, can wipe off the sin, by restoring four-fold, but he that cheats himself, poor soul! the sin will lie at his own door, and it will never be in his power to make himself restitution! no, no, I know better, that must be the crying, that is spoken of by Lazarus, Nicodemus, Judas, or some other prophet, I forget who now; alack! its many year ago, since I read the bible, no matter. I'll e'en go and inform the Collector, then I shall have one half to myself, and the other will go the President of the United States. They'll call me traitor and informer, but I don't care, let them laugh that wins, ha! ha! It's an old saying and a true one, aye, I have it! "One bird in hand is better far, than two that's in the bush,"—no, no, "than two that in bushes are." Aye, that's it! I remember it's so on my neighbour Simmond's sign. I love to make rhimes, when they jingle so cleverly, but here's two hundred and fifty thousand birds in the cage, and most of them pretty yellow birds! Oh! they'll make delightful music, and make me sing too! I mus'n't lose any time, no, indeed! (*He looks up*) I think this is the house, aye! (*knocks at the door several times, and calls*) Mr Collector! Mr Collector! (*Collector appears at the window, in his shirt and night-cap.*)

Col. Who's there! and what's your urgent business, disturbing my rest so soon in the morning?

Wash. Why, why sir, its business of very great importance!

Col. Importance, or not, I think you might have stay'd 'till day light.

Wash. I coud'n't sir—indeed I coud'n't!

Col. I'm not us'd to have my rest broke, at this unseasonable hour!

Wash. Sir, sir!—we'll satisfy you handsom'ly for this extraordinary inconvenience!

Col. (*Aside.*) That's speaking to the point!—Oh! very well!—very well!—what is the business, sir?

Wash. Why, why, sir! I have an information, to lay before you, concerning a chest of treasure——

Col. A chest of treasure? sir.

Wash. Yes! sir.

Col. A chest of treasure? I don't understand you, sir!

Wash. (*Aside.*) The deuce you dont? the fellow's stupid.—I say, a chest of treasure.

Col. Explain yourself, sir!

Wash. 'Tis already explain'd!—I tell you, sir! it's a chest of treasure that we dug out of the ground last night.

Col. Last night!—where?

Wash. Why, why, somewhere—but I hav'n't time to tell you now. Come down! sir—pray come!

Col. What! a large chest?

Wash. (*Aside.*) What a fool he is. Yes! a large chest and very heavy; I know I help'd to carry it, and it almost kill'd me.

Col. Why, how long is it?

Wash. Why, why! six foot long; as long as a coffin, (*aside*) and when it's emptied, I wish you were buried in it.

Col. Can you be serious, sir?

Wash. (*Aside.*) This fellow will exhaust all my patience. Yes, yes! I am, I am! myself and several others are concerned in it, and it grieves my conscience to cheat the President out of his lawful right, so, pray sir, seize it, seize it, instantly, for me and the President. I expect all concerned will be at my house directly to open and share it. Come, make haste sir, do!—Put the broad P on it, and then we shall be safe: you must act for me and the President, and we'll reward you handsomely.

Col. I'm afraid you're too sanguine, and it's all deception!

Wash. (*Aside*) What a cursed fool he is!—No! no! it an't, it an't; it's a real fact! here's occular demonstration! for this piece of money, (*shewing the piece*) dropt out of the chest when we took it out of the ground. Look here, sir! see it! see it!

Col. Say you so?

Wash. True, sir, true! pray be expeditious, do sir, do, I insist upon it.

Col. Well sir!—since you insist upon it, I must seize it.

Wash. I do! I do! my fidelity to the United States, obliges me to insist upon it.

Col. Remember your promise.

Wash. We'll satisfy you, nobly.

Col. I shall look to you alone, sir.

Wash. Very well! very well! I'll be your paymaster. (*Aside*) Since you're afraid to trust my part'ner. Come down, sir! do, do.

Col. I'll wait on you instantly.

Wash. He's cursedly afraid of trusting my part'ner. Ha! ha! ha! I shall soon let him know what a servant he has; a dilatory, suspicious dog! I'll have him turned out, as sure as he was put in. (*Collector enters the street.*) This way, sir! this way. Follow me, sir! quick! quick! or we shall be too late.

Col. Lead on, sir! lead on. (*Exeunt.*)

SCENE IV. *A Room in* WASHBALL's *House.*

(*Scene opens and discovers* TRUSHOOP, RACCOON, TROWELL, *and* BUCKRAM, *sitting on a chest, and* OLD GABRIEL *standing by.*)

(*Enter* HUM, PARCHMENT, QUADRANT, *and* RATTLETRAP.

Parch. Gabriel, where's your master?

Gab. Just stepp'd out.

Hum. Will he be in soon?

Gab. Aye—may be so.

Quad. Oh!—here he comes, but who the devil's that with him?

Parch. The collector! egad! This is what I didn't expect. (*Aside.*) It will not do to dupe him, we must let him into the secret.

Hum. Leave that to me.

(*Enter* COLLECTOR *and* WASHBALL.)

Hum. (*Takes the collector aside and says*) Sir, I am sorry you have been put to this trouble; it's a scheme of diversion only, please not to notice it; I'll acquaint you with the whole history of it when it is concluded.

Col. (*Aside*) Ha! ha! Just as I thought knowing your funny character.—Mr. Hum, your servant—gentlemen yours. (*Going.*)

Wash. Sir! sir! stay, pray do your duty!

Col. Sir,—its an affair too intricate for me at present, I must first advise with the States Attorney General.

Wash. You shan't go!—I insist upon it, I charge you in the President's name, seize it! seize it!

Col. I must first have advice, then I'll return again.

Wash. I forbid you to go at your peril! I'll inform the President, and you shall be hang'd for not doing your duty.

Col. I can't help that! (*Exit*)—(*Washball attempts to go after him, they stop him and he bawls*) Let me alone! let me alone!

Trus. Augh!—you cursed owld traytor, arn't you asham'd now, to be chating us after this way?

Quad. I never heard of such another villain.

Wash. O Lord,—oh!

Gab. (*Aside*) There's queer doings here.

Buck. Ye censemous auld skoondrel! ye turn'd een-former, and states-evedence, to get the ane half till yere sel, but yere oot noo, troth and I'ze a mine to leeghten yere heed by ane o yere luggs

Gab. (*Aside*) Worse and worse.

Wash. O Lord,—oh!

Rat. What did you tink, we are all fools to be cheated by you?

Hum. Nothing can equal this! open the chest, who knows but the States-attorney may be on our backs immediately?

Rat. Had I suspected this before, I could have summon'd a whole host of infernals, to have carried him away in a whirl-wind.

Trom. 'Tis a pity out you had, indeed.

Trus. Arra my deer! and give me a little bit of an order, and I'll fatch 'um in a jiffin

Rat. I shall have no more power, Mr. Trushoop, 'till the moon changes

Trus. Fath, an I'm sorry for that honey.

Wash. O Lord,—oh!

Parm. A traitor and an informer, gentlemen, of all mankind, are the most despicable of all wretches; you see gentlemen, the turpitude of that old curmudgeon's heart; after his most solemn oath of secrecy and honesty, he thinks nothing of betraying his best friends, (Judas like) and his own soul, for the sake of his body! without the least regard for a sacred and solemn oath!

Gab. (*Aside*) How he abuses my master.

Quad. Mr. Trushoop where's your adz? open the chest.

Trus. Augh my deer, and here we are, bote at your sharvifs.

Wash. (*Strives to prevent him, and calls*) Mr. Collector! Mr Collector!

Trus. Stand off, you old flubberdegullion, (*opening the chest, Hum, Parchment, Quadrant, and Rattletrap, holding Washball, he struggles to get from them, and bawls out*) where's the Collector? where's the Collector? touch it at your perils, you villains! I'll swear robbery against you! help Gabriel, help!

Gab (*Aside*) Lack-a-day, I believe they're going to rob my master! I would help him with all my heart, but my scuffling days are all over long ago.

Parch. Go on with your business gentlemen,—open the chest.—(*Trushoop, Trowell, Raccoon, and Buckram open the chest.*)

Wash. Touch it at your peril, I say. It belongs to me and my partner.

Trus Belongs to the devil, you tief—we'll soon see who'll fale the sharing it.

Gab. (*Aside*) I never see the like before.

Wash. Help—help!—murder—murder—fire—thieves—Betty, Betty, bring down the bags you made.—Run Gabriel for the Collector! Oh, oh, I'm just dead.

Gab Yes, I will, and the Constable too. Sorrow on me, but I believe they'll murder my master.

[*Exit Gabriel.*

Rac. Dare! de chest opens. (*They let Washball go, he runs towards the chest, the dupes all striving to get their shares.*)

Wash. Give me my share!—give me my share.

Trus. The devil a copper you tief

Buck. The deel a bawbie, ye shall ha' non.—(*In the scuffle they overse' the chest, push down Washball, and out tum-*

l'e the contents, the dupes looking at each other confused.)

Buck. Hoot mon—wha the deel's a this?—naething but stanes!—I ken we'll enaugh, wha it is—deil damme, but I'ze ha gen elman's satisfaction.

Rat. De tive.—It's de scheme of brudder Hum. I second your resolution, do you gib de chalenge Mr. Buckram.

Trow. Oh mercy!—(*Exit Hum, Parchment, Quadrant, and Rattletrap.*)

Tr.f. Augh hough!—fath, and we're all humbugged

Trow. Its all a cheat.

T'f. Augh! but this will be my heart breaking—by my sowl! and I've been made a fool for the futnre,—but I'll take care for the time to cum.

Rat. I didn't tink brudder Hum wou'd serve me so, but dan I'll inform de Lodge of dis—dare's Rattletrap too wid his stars and tings,—plague on dem all—and hab Mrs. Placket made de fool of me too, wid her conjur-book? I tink it can't be so nader, for she lobes me, or she wou'dn't call me her Cooney—cock-a-pigeon—cock-a-dandy, and all de fine tings, dad I'll—

Wash. Oh! I'm cheated—I'am abus'd, and made a fool of—I shall die, Oh! dear I shall die! (*lifting up his hands*) "poor Washball, disappointed Washball."

(*Enter* GABRIEL.)

Gab. (*Looking surpris'd with his hands clench'd, aside.*) What's all this! alack-a-day (*Hum, Parchment, Quadrant, and Rattletrap, peeping alternately, call Canoe!—Washball chasing them, and endeavouring to strike them with his cane,*) "get out of my house you villains," (*Canoe!*) "you dogs," (*Canoe!*) "you hell-hounds," (*Canoe!*) "O dear! O dear, I shall faint," (*Canoe!*) I'm dead! I'm dead," (*he sits down*) "Oh, Oh, Oh, (*Canoe!*) they laugh, and run off.

Trow. A miserable disappointment.

Iruf. Augh! fath and its all over now—this is the devils own works, and they're the devil's own children—and by my fowl, and they'll do grate pannance for all this.——(*Sings.*)

SONG XVIII. *To be Sung flow.*

Arra! what a fool was I?—by my fowl!—I think
I'll cry,
When I fpake of all this,—it encreafes my blifs;
'Twill kill me afore I die
Fath!—I'll now fhow my face, t'fcape all difgrace,
For me, they'll make a true jeft;
No more fhall my foes,
Drive me by my nofe,
In boggs, o'er my tofe,
Spiling brogues and hofe,
And carry the empty cheft.

Augh! fife now, my back is quite fore, becaze it
made me roar,
How it broke all my bones, pulling brick-batts and
ftones,
To the mill, from Wafhball's dure.
To hear the pane and fmart, I file in my hart,
My futt is both fick and lame;
With canoe! and bote,
I mudded my cote,
My wife will cut my trote,
The devil take the tote;
Augh! me—they'll make a grate game.

Buck. Deel dam 'em a'.

Rat. Dis, dis is my own fault, for being too cred'lous, I put too much truft in dem I tought my friends, and dey deceiv'd me. If I had been fatisfy'd wid my bus'nefs and follow'd a birtuous courfe of libe, den I fhould be happy to dis day, and hab nutting to trubble me, but now I hab feen my folly, and former wickednefs;

I will take de resolution to lede a new libe, and follow my bus'ness wid honesty and industry, and hab nutting to say to the banities and bexations, of dis wicked world, and from dis time my studdy shall be birtue, to de end of my libe

Buck. Confusion to the vullians!—I maun e'en gang and fut up my shap-board agen.

Trow. I can never face my wife after this.

Trus. Nor I, by St Patrick!—Augh, and she'll make no more suppers for poor Trushoop

Wash. Oh dear! I'm robb'd of my money, my health, and my ease, nothings left me now but to grieve and lament—how shall I procure my peace again? Let me see! a tend my bus'ness. What then? if a customer should laugh under the operation of my razor, egad! I should think he laughed at me, for being such a silly old dupe, and ten to one, but I might cut his throat for madness—dress a wig eigh? why I should think my blocks grinn'd at me! I'll instantly go and burn them all. If I should hear the noise of children in the street, I should think they bawl'd Canoe! Canoe! confound the word, I wou'd give five hundred pounds, it were high treason to utter it, then I would hang every one of those dogs. Oh dear! what can I do? If I rail against them publicly, I sha'l only have the cold comfort of "Its a piece of diversion only, nothing else,"—hellish diversion! suppose I should try to laugh it off? alas! alas! I can't do it, I shan't be in a laughing humor, these seven years I'am afraid.

(*Enter* MEANWELL *and* LUCY.)

Mean. Sir, we crave your blessing.—(*They kneel down.*)

Wash. Go to the devil! you dog.—(*Lifting up his cane, and stamping on the floor.*)

Trus Augh! and deer Lucy, sure and you're not married?

Lucy. It is so Mr. Trushoop. (*Aside*) Pray endeavour to pacify my uncle, pray gentlemen interpose.

Wash What does she say? eigh?

Trow. She says she's married, and begs your pardon.

Wash. Oh! the gipsey!—I shall run stark-mad! and how dare you do it without my consent? didn't I forbid you hussey? eigh!

Lucy Pray dear uncle, pardon us!

Wash. Thief like! break the laws, and then have the assurance to ask for pardon, eigh! no, no you can't plead ignorance, you knew the terms and consequences of disobeying me, now you've done it, and a pretty couple of beggars you are truly! arn't you? *(Aside.)* But stop! I'm going too fast, hold there, I forgot my own disappointment! the terms are void in themselves.—Well——

Rac. Come, come Mr. Washball, how can you be so angry wid dem, she's a pretty young ting.

Wash. O! lack-a-day! she's old enough to know better.

Trow Pardon them Mr. Washball.

Mean. Pray sir! pardon us.

Lucy. Pray uncle, give us your blessing.

Wash *(Aside.)* So, so, pardon and blessing too,—what comes next?

Truf. Let me intrate for 'um, fath, an they seem to be as well match'd, as a couple of coach horses.

Wash *(Aside.)* Now since I see the tide has turn'd against me, I mustn't be too hard with 'em, they are both young and I am old, and I may possibly want their assistance, before they will want mine.

Buck. Come, come mon, gie em yere blessin, troth she's, a sonsie, blinkin lass, and they're a bonnie pair

Wash O! lack-a-day!—I charge you both, tell me the truth!—are you really married?

Mean 'Tis really so, sir!

Lucy Dear uncle 'tis true—pray forgive!

Wash. Who married you?

Lucy. Parson Knottum, sir.

Wash. Eigh!—who?

Mean. Parson Knottum, sir.

Wash. Aye! I thought so! if he did it, there's no untying the knot, he's just such another fellow, as that a-a- what d'ye call him, a-a- Parson Holdfast. Well since 'tis so, God bless you both, (*crying*) but remember children, that bare walls make but giddy housewives.

Mean. Sir! we thank you for your kind condescension, and I must now inform you, that I have this day received a letter from Jamaica, giving an account of my uncle's death, inclosing a copy of his will, by which I understand he hath bequeathed me fifteen thousand pounds sterling in cash, with all his real and personal estate, consisting of four valuable windmill plantations, seven hundred and eighty-four negroes, a large quantity of very valuable plate, a part of which cash (as per bill of lading,) also, one hundred hogsheads of proof spirit and seventy-five hogsheads of prime sugar is remitted me, per the brig Welcome, captain Trusty.

Wash. I'm glad to hear it! my son—I'm glad to hear it! indeed I am! let me give you joy both of your spouse and fortune! (*Embraces him.*) It revives my drooping spirits! come hither Lucy, my good child! you're a good girl! indeed you are! and I wish you joy of your worthy husband and fortune. (*Embraces her.*) I'm rejoiced very much. (*Aside*) O dear! what a lucky turn for me.

Mean. Notwithstanding this flush of fortune, sir! I bear the same love for your niece and veneration for yourself as heretofore, and you may rest assured, sir! I shall make it my peculiar study to merit your esteem and her affection.

Wash. Aye! aye! 'tis very well my dear child, I believe you will, and indeed, I always loved you with a paternal affection, notwithſtanding ſometimes it hap'ned (unluckily when you were preſent) that ſomething had ruffled my temper, and I might not have ſhewn you the reſpect I otherwiſe wou'd have done, and which I was heartily ſorry for, when you were gone. But you muſt forgive and forget that, and in ſome meaſure attribute it to the imbecility and infirmity of old age, and to make amends, you have both my bleſſing, *(embraces them again)* and God bleſs you both, and may you live comfortably together, and ſee many happy days, and be bleſt with a train of dutiful children, like olive branches round about your table, to comfort you in your old age; "creſite et multiplicamini".—And, oh! that I, who have one foot in the grave and the other ſcarcely out, had but been contented, then, I ſhou'd have been happy in my old age and not have involved myſelf in this labyrinth of trouble and confuſion! But let it ſerve as a warning to others, not to liſten to idle ſchemes, nor give way to vain imaginations, which has prov'd ſo fatal to me! for, he whoſe deſires are unbounded, and is weak enough to liſten to artful deſigning men, ſtands upon a dangerous precipice, whoſe foundation muſt ſink and he inevitably periſh!

[*Sings ſlow and mournful.*

SONG XIX

Ah! who is me, poor wretched I?
With broken heart, and down caſt eyes!
To eaſe my mind, where ſhall I fly?
A prey to knaves, poor Waſhball dies!
Let future generations take
Example, by my diſmal fall!
Nor gods of gold, or idols make;
So ſhun the fate of poor Waſhball!

And now my good friends and fellow-sufferers, (*shakes hands with them,*) I expect you'll honor us with your company at dinner, and do my dear son, write a card of invitation to dinner, also, to the worthy Captain Trusty. We'll strive to make ourselves as merry as we can, and forget our folly and disappointment.— Gabriel call in the neighbours, and bring your fiddle and play for us, and we'll have a dance.

Gab. I will, I will, sorrow on me but I will! for we havn't had a dance since last Christmas. [*Exit Gab.*

Wash. In the mean time, my dear children, give me a song to sooth my troubled mind.

SONG XX.

Wash. Banish sorrow, welcome joy!
Let's strike up, the sprightly dance,
Mirth abound without alloy;
Tune your lutes, your pipes advance!
Sound your notes in lofty strains,
Join ye nymph's and jovial swains,
Banish care and be at rest,
Of disappointment, make the best.

Lucy. Room for joy, how blest am I,
In a husband and a friend?
Virtuous love shall never die,
Tho' our lives will surely end.
Virgins all example take,
Virtue love, for virtue's sake
Constant be—as turtle-dove,
Let your theme be virtuous love.

(*Enter* GABRIEL, *with his fiddle and neighbors, they strike up a country dance, after which* WASHBALL *says.*)

In search of treasure, we are led astray,
Believing fully, what deceivers say,
They tread unsure who 'gainst their senses run,
False steps pursue, and rush to be undone,
Curs'd by themselves! laugh'd at by ev'ry one.

[*Exeunt omnes to dinner.*

EPILOGUE.

T'Reclaim the vicious, is a noble deed!
The virtuous ſure, they leſs repentance need,
To knock down vice, it was our ſole intent,
And, if we've had ſucceſs, 'tis all we meant.
Th' avaricious wretch expos'd to view,
Ungrateful man!—more ſordid than a Jew!
Whoſe miſer'd ſoul—wrapt up in hoards of pelf,
No charity for any, but himſelf!
Ambition humbled,—virtuous love rewarded,
(For virtuous ſouls!—will ever be recorded.)
Expos'd the folly of the credulous,
Who put what ſenſe they have, out to a nurſe.
And vanity is check'd—whoſe pompous ſound,
With it's votaries levell'd with the ground.
To you our judges then, we muſt appeal,
Condemn or not—we ſatisfaction feel
In thinking, we have caus'd a reformation,
Among'ſt the dupes of this our congregation.

(Viewing the Audience thro' a glaſs.)

O! glorious ſight! how cloſe they ſqueeze and touch,
As thick as hops—or, like New-York ſtage-coach,
The Boxes ſhine, with brilliant belles and beaus!
The Pitt with critics, and Gallery o'erflows.
Each make remarks, well pleas'd, and with grimace,
They twiſt and ſcrew the muſcles of their face.
Hark! hark! they clap applauſe on ev'ry ſide,
Some mouths half open—others open'd wide;
Which ſhew the audience are gratify'd.
We thank you friends, thoſe marks of approbation;
Has ſaved our play, from what folks call damnation.
And ſince we've feaſted you with dainty diſhes!
With thanks! we'll now feaſt on,—the loaves and fiſhes.

CPSIA information can be obtained at www.ICGtesting.com
Printed in the USA
LVOW05s1149171013

357173LV00007B/593/P